EARTH
The Living Planet

EARTH
The Living Planet

Alexa Stace

Consulting Editor:
Dougal Dixon

EARTH—THE LIVING PLANET

Produced by

AND Cartographic Publishers Ltd
Alberto House
Hogwood Lane
Finchampstead
Berkshire RG40 4RF
United Kingdom

This edition published in the United States
of America by arrangement with Gareth Stevens,
Inc, Suite 201, 1555 RiverCenter Drive,
Milwaukee, W1 53212, USA.

ISBN 0-8368-2490-3 (special edition)

10 9 8 7 6 5 4 3 2 1

LIBRARY OF CONGRESS
CATALOGING-IN-PUBLICATION DATA

Stace, Alexa.
    Earth, the living planet/ by Alexa Stace: consulting editor
Dougal Dixon.
        p.   cm. –
    Includes index.
    Summary: Examines the various physical features and
    forces that shape the planet and discusses the impact of
    humans on the environment.
    ISBN 0-8368-2490-3
    1. Earth--Juvenile literature. [1. Earth. 2.Physical
    geography.] 1. Dougal Dixon. 11. Title. 111.Series.
    08631.4.S657   2000
    550--dc21   98-27458
                                                    CIP
                                                    AC

Color origination by Job Color srl, Italy

Printing by Centro Grafico Ambrosiano srl, Italy

Contents

Introduction

SINCE THE dawn of civilization people have been trying to understand their own world. The earliest maps, produced

by the Ancient Greeks, showed the islands and coastlines of the Mediterranean Sea – the limit of known travel for their galleys and sailing ships.

The study of mathematics, astronomy, geology and the other sciences brought about more and more accurate surveying, and as the world became better known in the Middle Ages the maps of the Earth became gradually more detailed and more meaningful.

In modern times the development of air travel enabled us to see, for the first time, our living landscape from above. The shapes of islands, the courses of rivers, the layouts of cities could now be seen directly. It was even possible for astronauts,

OUR EARTH – THE LIVING PLANET

flying high enough, to detect the actual curvature of the horizon.

Now we live in the Space Age. In the late 1960s the first manned expeditions to the Moon brought us back photographs of our own planet as a sparkling jewel set in the empty, star-studded darkness of infinite space – the entire planet on a single photograph frame.

We can now send satellites into orbit to look down on our own world, with a whole array of cameras, scanners and sensors. Computers can analyse data and present it in the form of photographs, altered so that the false colors produced can reveal surface features invisible in normal light. As well as showing us just what our world looks like, these techniques have had

far-reaching effects on all kinds of environmental studies, including agriculture, forestry,

WATER AND AIR –
IT HELPS TO MAKE
US UNIQUE

IMAGING THE EARTH

The photographs taken from space and published in this book have either come from satellites, such as Landsat, or have been taken by astronauts from the Space Shuttle.

Space imaging has come a long way since John Glenn first snapped a few pictures from his capsule on February 20, 1962. Nowadays it is possible to photograph objects less than 3ft wide from near space, "see" under desert sands, and find long-lost rivers.

Conventional photography

False-colour image

PICTURES IN O'S AND 1'S
When a signal is beamed down from a satellite to a satellite dish, it is then conveyed as digital data along special telephone lines to a computer.

Once captured and "cleaned up", the data can be made available to the public in a number of ways as either natural or false color images.

LANDSAT

AROUND THE EARTH IN 90 MINUTES
The Space Shuttle – actually three different craft – has carried cameras since the early missions in the 80s. The photography is usually hand-held, using conventional cameras. Sometimes special infra-red film is used.

SPACE SHUTTLE

0010011011
1000111011
0101111011
1011001101

urban planning and the location of mineral and water resources.

Diagrams in textbooks have always been valuable in presenting the theory behind geographic features. Now we can back up those diagrams with images from space. We can see just how a river follows its course from the mountains to the sea; we can see the march of sand dunes across an entire desert; we can see the different kinds of coral produced as an island chain ages. The elegance, the simplicity, the complexity of the Earth's natural processes, and

the human modification of them, can now be seen directly.

We can present a

snapshot album of our own home!

Dougal Dixon,
Consulting Editor

FIRE AND HEAT –
NATURE AT ITS
MOST
SPECTACULAR

PART ONE

A living planet

The Earth in action –
how movements in the Earth's crust,
its atmosphere, and even outer space,
shape the planet

Earth in space

See also:
- **The air around us** p14
- **Moving plates** p18
- **Spreading rifts** p22
- **Building mountains** p24

WHERE WE ARE IN SPACE

The nine planets of the solar system are either small and rocky, or huge and made of gas. The Earth is the largest of the five known rocky planets, four of which lie close to the Sun. It is only one-eighth the diameter of Jupiter, the largest of the gas giants.

9 Pluto

8 Neptune

7 Uranus

6 Saturn

5 Jupiter

4 Mars

3 Earth

2 Venus

1 Mercury

THE SUN is the life-giving force for our planet, and the distance of the Earth from the Sun is essential for the continuation of life.

The "ecosphere" is the region around the sun with a suitable temperature to sustain life. Inside the inner boundary would be too hot; outside the outer boundary would be too cold. Earth is at the mid-point, with Venus at the inner edge and Mars at the outer. Nowhere else in the solar system is able to support life as we know it. Although the Moon is a similar distance from the sun, it lacks an atmosphere, so the average temperature is 3°F, compared with Earth's 59°F.

ORBITS IN SPACE

The numbers refer to the position of the planets in orbit in relation to the Sun.

EARTHRISE, DECEMBER 22 1968

Left:

As Apollo VIII orbited around the Moon on its pre-landing mission, the astronauts took this picture showing our planet rising above the Moon's horizon. The Moonscape is lit orange by the rays of the Sun which is behind the passing space capsule.

ONE THEORY

The making of Earth has many theories.

One theory is that a star was hit by a passing asteroid.

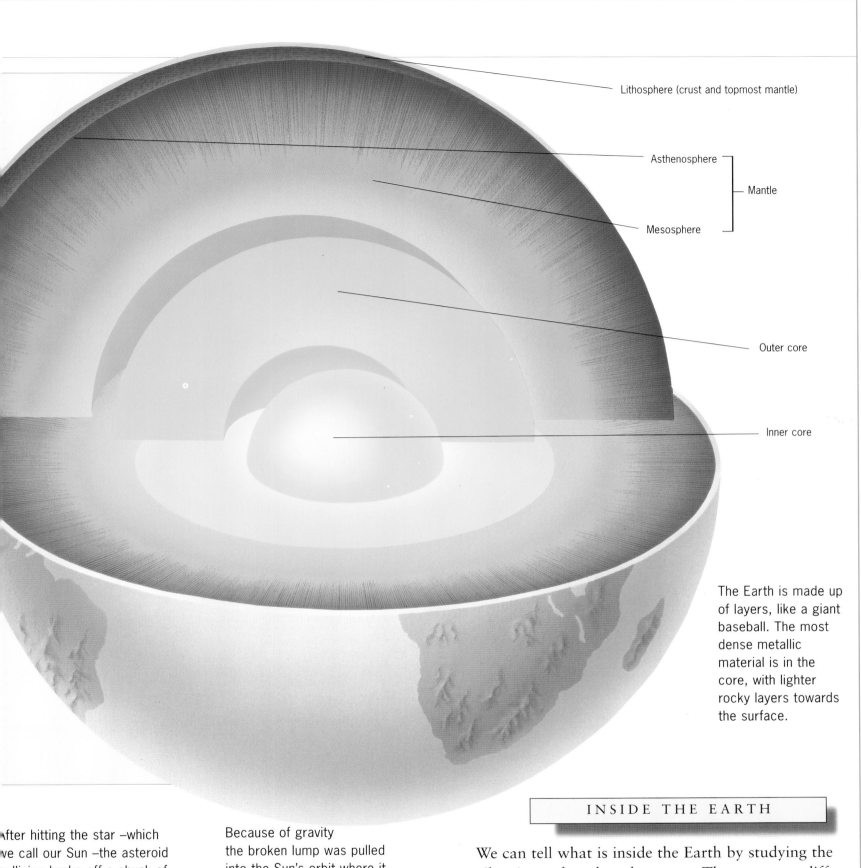

Lithosphere (crust and topmost mantle)

Asthenosphere

Mesosphere

Mantle

Outer core

Inner core

The Earth is made up of layers, like a giant baseball. The most dense metallic material is in the core, with lighter rocky layers towards the surface.

After hitting the star –which we call our Sun –the asteroid collision broke off a chunk of stellar debris. This in turn was flung off the Sun.

Because of gravity the broken lump was pulled into the Sun's orbit where it cooled down and later became a proto-earth.

INSIDE THE EARTH

We can tell what is inside the Earth by studying the vibrations of earthquake waves. There are two different kinds of vibrations – one makes a back-and-forth movement and another makes a side-to-side movement. The first can pass through layers of solid and liquid, but the second can only pass through solids.

From these studies we know that the center of the Earth – the inner core – is solid. This is surrounded by a liquid outer core. The main bulk of the Earth is is the solid rocky mantle, which has a squashy area – the asthenosphere – near the top. The crust, which is the only part we can sample directly, forms a kind of very thin "rind" around the outside.

The air around us

See also:
- **Fallen stars** *p30*
- **Rivers** *p38*
- **... and deltas** *p42*
- **Holes in the sky** *p76*

Below:
This famous image, taken during one of the Apollo missions in the late 1960s, shows the effect of light splitting into its component parts–refracting–in the atmosphere.

Sun rays strike the atmosphere and are split into various parts.

THE ATMOSPHERE is the outermost "shell" of the Earth's structure. It is composed of a mixture of gases which envelop the whole globe. At first, the atmosphere contained a poisonous mixture of gases such as hydrogen, carbon dioxide, and methane. But as plants evolved they absorbed much of the carbon dioxide and produced oxygen, so that gradually the atmosphere became as it is today – a mixture of gases which is able to support animal life.

THE EARTH'S BLANKET

Without the atmosphere the Earth would be unbearable. The side facing the sun would roast in the heat, while the other side would be freezing. The atmosphere acts like insulation. During the day it filters out most of the harmful rays from the sun, but allows sunlight through. At night, it traps warmth at the Earth's surface and prevents it from radiating into space. But with a different mixture of gases too much heat would be trapped at the surface, producing the "greenhouse effect."

PARTS OF A RAY
1. Most infrared rays pass through the atmosphere.
2. Most ultraviolet rays are reflected away.
3. Light reaches the surface, but also reflects back.
4. The infrared rays that reach the surface are bounced back.
5. Some of the reflected infrared radiation is trapped in the atmosphere.

Right
A meteorite burns up as it hits the Earth's atmosphere. Only on rare occasions do they penetrate this shield.

1

2

3

4

5

LIFE CYCLES

The Earth is a dynamic system, with something always happening. Nearly all the chemicals that make up the Earth and the living things on it have been here since the Earth was first formed, some 15 billion years ago.

When rocks form, they do so from fragments of rocks that existed before. Eventually the new rocks decay or are broken down, and the remains form another generation of rocks. It is the same in the living systems. All the substances in an animal's or a plant's life cycle are reused over and over again.

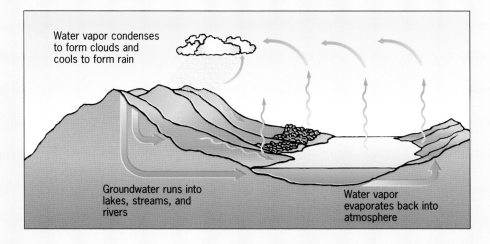

Water vapor condenses to form clouds and cools to form rain

Groundwater runs into lakes, streams, and rivers

Water vapor evaporates back into atmosphere

Left:
The atmoshere is colored by pollutants, suspended dust, and other matter. Here the sky has been turned golden red by the dust generated by the 1991 volcanic explosion of Mount Pinatubo in the Philippines. The dust cloud affected a large portion of the Earth's atmosphere, much like the gigantic volcanic explosion of nearby Krakatao in 1883 when ash encircled the whole Earth.

Oxygen in the atmosphere falls onto Earth in rain and is breathed in by animals on land

Photosynthesis by plants on land and by marine animals in the sea passes back oxygen into the atmosphere

THE WATER CYCLE
What makes Earth unique is that water is freely available at the surface. It exists in three forms: liquid, solid, or vapor.

Water travels in the oceans, and is evaporated by the sun into vapor. The vapor condenses into clouds of droplets which fall as rain.

The water flows on the surface or through the rocks to emerge as springs. Streams flow downhill, and so water returns eventually to the oceans as rivers.

Along this route water is used by animals, plants and man. It is absorbed into their bodies, and returned back to the Earth when its work is done.

CARBON AND OXYGEN CYCLES
Life is based on the workings of organic chemistry. This involves the build-up and breakdown of complex carbon-based molecules.

Oxygen and carbon are constantly moving about in this system. Carbon is the foundation of all plant and animal life, while oxygen enables the living organisms to breathe.

Carbon dioxide is given off into the atmosphere and breathed in by plants to aid photosynthesis

Decaying plants and animal waste feeds soil

Earth movements

See also:
- **Moving plates** *p18*
- **Volcano!** *p20*
- **Spreading rifts** *p22*
- **Building mountains** *p24*

Hot magma rises up and sometimes escapes through cracks and volcanoes in the Earth's surface.

Underneath the Earth's thin shell lies an enormous pulsating mass of hot and cool liquid rock on which our continents float. In this computer model, red is hot rock and blue is cool. The flows have been shown separately for clarity.

Cooling magma flows down to the center of the Earth to be re-heated.

HUGE SECTIONS, or "plates," of the Earth's hard outer layers produce massive forces as they float on partly molten rock.

The slow movement of these plates – no more than about 5 inches a year – affects the shape of the continents. And the forces produced as the plates collide or move apart are responsible, over many millions of years, for the formation of mountains, volcanoes, underwater canyons, and earthquakes.

Volcanoes are formed more dramatically. Molten rock called "magma" is forced through cracks in the Earth's crust. The magma cools quickly into the solid rock of volcanic mountains.

Cracks on the ocean floor, oozing molten lava, build new sea floor, while the rubbing together of the plates causes earthquakes to take place.

PANGAEA 250M YEARS AGO

HOW THE WORLD HAS CHANGED.

The Earth today is very different from what it was like 250 million years ago. Then it was one large landmass, known as Pangaea, with a single ocean – the Tethys Ocean. Gradually, over millions of years, Pangaea split apart in a process known as "continental drift" into the globe that we recognize today.

JURASSIC EARTH 200M YEARS AGO

CRETACEOUS EARTH 150M YEARS AGO

Left:
Active volcanoes are among the most spectacular sights on Earth. This photograph, taken in Hawaii, shows molten rock from inside the Earth's crust oozing out of cracks and slowly cooling.

THE EARTH TODAY

OUR MOVING WORLD

The Earth's upper layer is made up of six major plates. and a few smaller ones. Many plates consist of both ocean floor and dry land.

   The diagram shows the main plate boundaries, the edges where the Earth's crust is weakest. Most volcanoes and earthquakes occur on these edges.

Key

The main plate boundaries

The direction of movement

 Cocos plate   Caribbean plate ❸ Arabian plate ❹ Philippine plate

Moving plates

See also:
- **Earth movements** *p16*
- **Volcano!** *p20*
- **Spreading rifts** *p22*
- **Building mountains** *p24*

SHALLOW SEA
The North Sea rests on a low, submerged continental shelf. This sea-bed is slowly expanding east–west with the rest of the Eurasian Plate, creating the rock structures that form the North Sea oil fields.

TWO-WAY STRETCH
The north–south rift valleys of the Rhône and the Rhine rivers are the result of the European Plate being stretched and torn as the Adriatic continues to push it eastwards.

SHRINKING OCEAN
More than 100 million years ago, the mighty Tethys Ocean separated two great continents – the Eurasian Plate and the Indo-Australian Plate. After the collision of the plates some 45 million years ago, all that remains of this ocean are the Mediterranean, the Caspian Sea and the Black Sea.

IBERIA STRIKES OUT
Spain and Portugal have split away from France, moved south and swung around. This has opened up the Bay of Biscay and crunched up the land between, forming the Pyrenees mountains.

MOVING ISLANDS
Plate movement has slowly pulled the islands of Corsica and Sardinia away from the underside of France and Italy, and into their present position.

Above:
Europe, with its valleys, mountains, bays, and islands, is a perfect example of a continent created by tectonics.

THE BARE BONES of all the continents are the result of plate movements, past and present. Colliding plates twist up mountain chains, diverging plates wrench continents apart, and active plate boundaries are the sites of volcanoes and earthquakes.

The shapes of the continents may seem random, but they all represent the legacy of the worldwide movement of the Earth's surface.

SWINGING LANDS

Europe has a solid heart of ancient rock, surrounded by crumpled mountain ranges of younger rock.

These younger rocks have been shaped by continuous plate movement. In the last few ten millions of years the African Plate has moved north, colliding with Europe, squeezing out the ocean between, and throwing up mountain ranges along the edge. Now Africa is moving east, stretching out the fabric of Europe east–west.

These rocks were built up about 400 million years ago.

The Baltic shield of ancient rocks is partly buried under new rock which forms Belarus, Poland, and much of Eastern Europe.

These rocks were built up about 300 million years ago.

The Atlas Mountains in Morocco, the Appennines in Italy, the Alps, and the Carpathian Mountains in Eastern Europe have all been twisted into a continuous s-shape as the two continents – Europe and Africa – ground past one another.

These rocks were built up about 50 million years ago and are the youngest in Europe. They are also the most earthquake prone and volcanically active.

Today Australia has swung around in the opposite direction.

WALTZING MATILDA, WALTZING MATILDA

Australia was originally part of Gondwana, the southern super-continent which also included Antarctica, India, Africa, and South America. Gondwana began to break up about 65 million years ago, splitting into the various continents as we now know them. Australia was the last to move, breaking off from Antarctica about 50 million years ago and drifting northwards. It is still moving. Some day it will collide with the mainland of Asia and vast mountain ranges like the Himalayas will be thrown up in between.

Australia's progress north, as part of Gondwana and as a single continent, can be plotted by examining the magnetism rocks formed at certain times.

Right :
Marsupials, like this opossum, probably spread from the Americas to Australia via Antarctica, at the time these continents were all joined together.

50 million years ago Australia was upside down after separating from Antarctica.

Volcano!

See also:
- **Earth movements** *p16*
- **Moving plates** *p18*
- **Spreading rifts** *p22*
- **Shake, rattle, and roll** *p26*

THE GREATEST FORCES on Earth can be unleashed when a volcano erupts – or it could be a small stream of molten magma slowly cooling into rock. Such is the unpredictable nature of volcanic activity. This is why volcanoes are so dangerous.

The most famous eruption occurred in Italy in 79AD when Mount Vesuvius smothered the Roman towns of Pompeii and Herculaneum in hot ash. In 1883 Krakatao, an island volcano east of Java, blew apart and disappeared overnight, and in 1991 Mount Pinatubo in the Philippines produced the greatest volcanic explosion of this century.

THE TWO TYPES OF VOLCANO

Cone volcanoes, formed by explosive andesitic magma, are to be found in the Pacific's "Ring of Fire."

Shield volcanoes are less explosive, and have gently spreading slopes, typical of Hawaiian volcanoes.

The white-hot ash and dust, lubricated by expanding gases – pyroclastic flow – rushed downward at 100mph and with the blast swept away 497 square miles of prime timber.

Above:
As the Space Shuttle Endeavour passed over the Kamchatka Peninsula, just north of Japan, it observed the belching smoke plume of the Klyuchevskaya volcano. An andesitic volcano, this September 1994 explosion shot smoke and ash 36,949 ft into the atmosphere. Winds then carried the debris over 640 miles. Air traffic had to fly longer routes to avoid the ash-cloud.

It is one of a group of 20 volcanoes along the peninsula, situated on the Pacific "Ring of Fire." They erupt, on average, three to five times each year.

WHEN WASHINGTON BLEW ITS TOP

On the morning of 18 May, 1980 Mount St Helens erupted. Its summit collapsed, the sides of the volcano burst outward triggering landslides, and a searingly hot ash cloud shot upward for almost 12 miles. Within two weeks this cloud had encircled the Earth.

During its eruption, the volcano ejected a cubic mile of airborne debris and lost 1,300ft of its original height. Sadly, eight geological observers also lost their lives after being caught by the blast.

The blast was the first volcanic eruption in the continental United States for over 60 years.

APRIL, 1980
BEFORE

The mountain first exploded sideways, bulging outward. The force was the equivalent of a 10 megaton bomb–500 times more deadly than the bomb that destroyed Hiroshima in 1945.

18 MAY, 1980
DURING

The shock-wave can easily be seen around the volcano's slopes. Within the blast area all the trees had been felled in the same direction.

JUNE, 1980
AFTER

Right:
The aftermath of the cataclysmic explosion and blast wave.

Spreading rifts

See also:
- **Earth movements** *p16*
- **Moving plates** *p18*
- **Volcano!** *p20*
- **Building mountains** *p24*

Below:
The western coastline of Africa matches that of South America, from which it split 120 million years ago.

Nᴇᴡ ᴘʟᴀᴛᴇꜱ form as molten rock from the Earth's interior wells up along cracks and solidifies. This usually happens under the sea, producing the ocean ridges. But sometimes it occurs beneath a continent, causing it to split up and break apart. This is what is happening to Africa.

A satellite photograph clearly shows the third crack in the African Plate – a string of underwater volcanoes, and the volcanic belt of the Cameroons.

OUT OF AFRICA

When Pangaea broke up into today's continents, it did so along rifts. Africa proves this. The coastlines form a jigsaw fit with those of the other continents it split from. What's more, Africa is still splitting. The Rift Valley system, which stretches from the Red Sea down to Mozambique, shows where the split is happening.

A rift usually starts as a rise in the Earth's crust from which three cracks radiate out. Two cracks develop the main rift movement, while the third is less active.

RIFT VALLEY SECTION

Vertical cracks (faults) where rock-masses have slipped down

Rift valley, often with lake on valley floor

One side of the rift valley slips down against the fault of the other

Below:
The floor of the Rift Valley in Ethiopia (the Afar Triangle) matches the coastline of Yemen to the north-east.

MT KENYA
This volcano is one of the many volcanoes in the area. Most are now extinct. Some have glaciers even though they are on the Equator.

MADAGASCAR
This large island was once joined to Africa. It is now travelling towards India.

RED SEA RIFT
The opposite shores of the Red Sea match one another. They only overlap in the area of the Afar Triangle, where three cracks diverge.

RIFT LAKES
The great lakes that can be seen from space mark out the Great Rift Valley in East Africa. They are the deepest lakes on the continent.

UNDERSEA BACKBONE

New plates are constantly being created along the under-water ocean ridges. Molten rock, known as magma, wells to the surface along a rift and solidifies, forming mountains running parallel to the ridge. This then pulls apart and forms another rift, and more material wells up and solidifies. Over the years this material builds up into plates that then move away from one another. The youngest part of the plate is closest to the rift, and the oldest is the furthest away.

Left:
The rift along the center of the Mid-Atlantic Ridge. Parallel mountain ridges along each side show where new crust is deposited.

Building mountains :

See also:
Earth movements *p16* • **Volcano!** *p20*
Moving plates *p18* • **Spreading rifts** *p22*

WHEN TWO CONTINENTAL plates collide, it is like a motor accident – but instead of lasting for a few fractions of a second, the collision takes place over millions of years. The stresses and strains are enormous. The forces have to escape, and in the only direction possible – upward. In this way mountains are born.

FOUR MAJOR KINDS OF MOUNTAINS

FOLD MOUNTAINS

BLOCK MOUNTAINS

VOLCANOES

DOME MOUNTAINS

Left:
The spiky profile of a young mountain. The most youthful rock lies at the top of the peak. A mere 50 million years ago these rocks would have been mud and sand at the bottom of the sea. This peak is in the French Alps near the border with Italy.

Mountain shapes have been split into four distinctive types. All of them have been formed through the actions of heat and pressure, and weathered by wind and water.

THE MAKING OF THE HIMALAYAS

Above:
The Indian sub-continent as viewed by an orbiting satellite.

About 165 million years ago, the Indo-Australian plate started to move north-ward towards the central Asian plate. As it hit the older and harder rocks, parts of the younger Indian Plate rose up and over the Asian Plate. At the same time, parts of it were pushed down into the Earth's crust.

Today, the Himalayas are still rising more than quarter of an inch a year. In a million years time they could be 16,000ft higher – even allowing for some weathering.

TIBETAN PLATEAU

...ay from the point of ...pact the rocks are ...mpled ...into

"Young" mountains rise up at the point of impact

Direction of movement.

At the point of impact, rocks slip and slide under great pressure. This causes heat to build up and the rock to *metamorphose*, or change, into new rock types. It is at these points that earthquakes may also occur.

Oceanic crust is not as strong as the continental crust with which it collides.

Himalayan mountains ...ain most of the ...'s peaks higher ...25,000ft.

The thinner oceanic crust dives under the older, harder continental rock and melts to form new rocks hundreds of miles below the Earth's surface.

Everest, the world's highest point, rises 29,118ft above sea level.

INDIAN SUB-CONTINENT

YOUNG AND OLD

"YOUNG" MOUNTAINS
When the shapes of mountains are sharp and jagged, they are termed "young." This is Mount Everest.

"OLD" MOUNTAINS
The action of natural weathering gradually wears down the sharp edges of the rocks so that they take on a rounded look. At this point they become known as "old" mountains like these in central Asia.

This three-dimensional computer model of India shows the Himalayan range in exaggerated perspective to emphasize the massive collision of the two plate boundaries that created the Himalayas. Compare it with the inset picture on the far left.

Shake, rattle, and roll

See also:
- **Earth movements** *p16*
- **Moving plates** *p18*

Right and far right:
The San Andreas Fault as it appears a few thousand feet above the Mojave Desert, which borders the Landers area. At other points it even bisects highways and road systems.

EARTHQUAKES are perhaps the most deadly of all the catastrophes that can strike the human race. It is known that over one million quakes shake the earth every year, but most are hardly ever felt.

When two layers of moving rock stick, instead of slide, forces are built up so that eventually the energy is released with explosive force. The point at which this happens is called the "epicenter." Energy flows out, like the ripples on a pond after a stone has been thrown into it. These waves, which take different forms, can travel through the rock in seconds. The recent 1989 San Francisco earthquake shook an area of 621 square miles, from southern Oregon to Los Angeles.

Earthquake epicenter

Landers township

Main fault lines

Above:
On 28 June 1992, Landers, in California, was shaken by an earthquake of 7.3 magnitude. This computer enhancement shows shock-waves rippling outward from the quake's epicenter.

THE "BIG ONE"

For almost a century Californians have been living in dread of the "Big One," an earthquake that will match the 7.7 magnitude shock that toppled San Francisco in 1906. The quake of 1989 in Northern California suggested that all would be far from well when the next large tremor strikes. Experts have warned that, when the time comes for another tremor, it will be preceded by a "seismic silence." Reliable earthquake prediction is still a long way away.

In certain earthquake-prone countries like Italy and Turkey new construction must be of an "earthquake-

THE FAULT LIES IN THE GROUND

There are three main kinds of fault found in rock strata. Each is as deadly as the others. Coupled with the wave-like action of seismic shocks, it is little wonder that the earth shakes and twists.

Normal fault

Strike-slip fault

Thrust fault

SAN FRANCISCO 1906

SAN FRANCISCO 1989

SAN FRANCISCO
Much of the 1989 destruction was caused to buildings sited on land reclaimed after the 1906 earthquake.

SAN ANDREAS FAULT
The fault line can clearly be seen from space as it crosses the San Francisco Bay. To the left of the picture the fault is particularly visible just above the white-shored cape known as the Point Reyes National Seashore.

proof" standard. Reinforced concrete is now suspect as under certain conditions it can crumble. In the US engineers are experimenting with frameworks that sway rather than crack, rubber cushions to separate buildings from the ground, and computer-controlled pistons to counteract the earthquake's movement.

Fire almost inevitably follows an earthquake, and emergency services plan accordingly.

The rock story

See also:
- **Volcano!** *p20*
- **Spreading rifts** *p22*
- **Rivers** *p38*
- **... and deltas** *p42*

As OLD AS THE HILLS – we think of the Earth's crust as indestructible. But in fact the rocks that make up the mountains and hills are constantly being broken down and rebuilt.

They may have been rebuilt after being melted and resolidified. They may be compressed and "cooked" into completely new types of rock. Or they may be broken down by erosion and fused together into different kinds of rock types.

This constant renewing of the Earth's surface is known as the rock cycle.

Above:
The Grand Canyon, carved out by the Colorado River, is 217 miles long.

Erosion over three million years has laid bare the geological history of the rock in a layer more than one mile deep.

Below:
These basalt rock columns in Northern Ireland are formed from solidified lava that came from a now extinct volcano. Basalt is an igneous rock.

HOW ROCKS ARE FORMED

Rocks are gradually broken down and eroded by weathering. The debris is slowly washed away and piles up to form a deep layer of sediment.

Through time, this layer of sediment is compressed and compacted by the weight of further layers laid down. Water passing through the sediment lays down minerals between the rock particles, causing chemical and physical changes that cement the particles into a solid mass.

The end result is sedimentary rock, one of the three kinds of rock. Sedimentary rock is formed in horizontal layers, called strata. These become visible when the rock is exposed by river erosion, as in the Grand Canyon, or when hills formed of sedimentary rocks, like the Appalachians, are worn away.

The other two kinds of rock are igneous rock – formed from magma – and metamorphic rock, shaped and compressed by the Earth's forces from pre-existing rock.

Metamorphic rock is created when rock buried in the heart of a mountain chain becomes compressed and heated, perhaps through the movement of tectonic plates. The mineral crystals in the rock break down and realign to give new rocks with a different texture. Marble, shale, and schist are all metamorphic rocks.

Right :
Marble is an example of metamorphic rock. This rock was once sedimentary limestone until pressure and heat set about altering it. The many beautiful colors of marble come from impurities in the original limestone.

BORN IN FIRE

Molten material within the Earth – magma – may squeeze to the surface and erupt through volcanoes or ooze out onto the ocean floor. The magma will cool and solidify into a fine-grained, extrusive igneous rock.

If the magma cools and solidifies before it reaches the surface, it produces an intrusive igneous rock. This rock is coarse-grained, with big crystals of minerals in it, such as granite.

SANDS OF TIME

The different types of sedimentary rock that exist, along with the structures and fossils embedded in them, help us to work out the history of the Earth.

ROCK TYPE
Coarse sediment, such as a shingle beach, becomes the coarse sedimentary rock conglomerate. Sand gives sandstone. Finer silts and mud give siltstone and shale. Chemicals deposited on a seafloor give limestone.

SEDIMENTARY STRUCTURES
Silt drying out in the sun shrivels into cracks, and these can be preserved in the siltstone. Ripples in shore sand and pits formed by rainfall can also be preserved – eyewitnesses to ancient climates.

LIFE OF THE PAST
The remains of animals, birds, and plants that lived and died when layers of sediment were laid down are often buried and preserved as fossils.
From the evidence of these fossils, we can plot the history of life on Earth.

Right :
A massive amount of silt and sand is transported by rivers. It is then deposited in estuaries and deltas, like the Mekong in Vietnam.

Fallen stars

See also:
- **Earth in space** *p12*
- **Volcano!** *p20*
- **Building mountains** *p24*
- **Shake, rattle, and roll** *p26*

The Earth has been bombarded by rocky debris from space – comets and meteorites – ever since the planet was formed. Most meteorites burn up in the atmosphere, but a few are large enough to reach the ground. In recent years there have been a few "near misses," such as when the comet Shoemaker-Levy tore itself apart going round Jupiter in 1994. What would be the effect on Earth of such a strike? Statistically, it is only a matter of time before another comet threatens our planet.

Above:
Satellite view showing sooty impact site of a possible comet landing on Greenland in December 1997. Comets are made up from "dirty snow" and ice, while meteorites are solid rock.

Right:
The massive crater at Manicouagan in Quebec Canada. The crater is 47 miles wide and is thought to be 210 million years old.

The meteorite struck the ancient rock of the Canadian Shield, so the crater has not been destroyed by plate movement.

YUCATAN IMPACT SITE

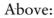

Radins of iridium deposit marking extent of asteroid impact

THE BIGGEST HIT YET?

65 million years ago, something wiped out the dinosaurs, and most other life on Earth as well. The culprit was probably a vast meteorite that landed in Chicxulub, Mexico, forming a crater 110 miles in diameter. The dust and gases sent high into the atmosphere would have changed the climate for a long time, making the Earth cold and dark. Plants could not have survived, and animals would have starved to death.

HOW TO MAKE AN IMPRESSION

A meteorite rips into the surface of the Earth with explosive impact, melting a large crater and blasting out debris. The craters on the Moon look similar.

1 Meteorite enters at an angle, and so is not deflected by the Earth's atmosphere.

2 Rocky "ejecta" is thrown out of the crater made by the colliding meteorite. The heat of the impact fuses and transforms rocks over the whole collision area.

3 A high-profiled edge is thrown up around the crater. Over time this erodes away.

Dust settles into the impact hole made by the meteorite. A mountain in the center is formed of rock pulled up by the explosion.

Below:
Meteor Crater in Arizona was made about 10,000 years ago. It is more than 650 ft deep and three quarters of a mile in diameter. An impact like this on a city is unimaginable.

Squashed forests

See also:
- ...lakes p40
- ...and deltas p42
- Changing coasts p62

Below:
The swamp forests of the coal ages were similar to the modern delta swamps of the Equatorial rainforest.

COAL IS FOSSILIZED PLANT material. For millions of years swamp forests on Earth absorbed the energy of the sun and the carbon dioxide of the atmosphere as they grew. When the trees died they were buried by other plant material and did not rot away, due to the lack of oxygen. After millions of years of compression the carbon in this material turned into coal. Nowadays, when we burn coal we release the energy that was stored all those millions of years ago.

Left:
A fossil leaf, typical of the plants that formed the Carboniferous Period forest.

As vegetation dies off it sinks into the muddy swamp water. Layers of this organic debris build up over the centuries.

HOW A SWAMP BECOMES COAL

A layer of dead plant material is buried in river sand. Over millions of years this layer is compressed as other layers are formed on top of it. As the sand turns to sandstone, the plant material loses much of its hydrogen and oxygen, and the carbon becomes more condensed. The greater the proportion of carbon the higher the grade of coal.

Peat is formed as the dead vegetation loses its moisture and becomes more compressed.

COAL IN NORTH AMERICA

Most of the world's coal was formed in the Carboniferous period, about 300 million years ago.

At this time newly formed mountain ranges were eroding, spreading sediment across the shallow seas round about. This produced large areas of delta, which in turn were covered with swamp forests.

Coal from this period is found in eastern North America, in Pennsylvania and Ohio. Lignite – Permian coal – is found in the Great Plains and further west into the Rockies.

COAL ZONES IN THE USA

Key

Carboniferous outcrops ■

Permian outcrops ☐

Above:
Many coalfields, such as at Black Mesa in the US Arizona Desert, come from the Permian period, which is more recent. Such coal is of a lower grade.

When these fields are close to the surface they can be mined by the opencast method.

s millions of years
ass, peat becomes
oal through a
rocess of
ompression and
hemical change

Deep shaft coal mine

Opencast coal mine

Black gold

See also:
- **...lakes** *p40*
- **...and deltas** *p42*
- **Changing coasts** *p62*

Above:
Oil and gas move through porous rocks, usually floating upward through the groundwater. They are lost at the surface unless they are caught in rock structures called traps. The Zagros Mountains of Iran (above) and other areas of the Middle East are full of these traps, giving rise to the great oil industry of the area.

Left:
Oil refinery tanks and pipelines in Saudi Arabia.

MUCH OF TODAY'S economy in the West is based on oil. Oil is used as a fuel and a power source, and it is also a valuable raw material: a vast range of plastics are made from oil.

Like coal, oil is a fossil fuel, formed from the remains of tiny sea creatures that were buried on the sea floor under layers of sediment where lack of oxygen prevented the normal process of decay. Bacterial action and heat from within the Earth broke down these substances into a series of carbon compounds, trapped within the rock underground.

These carbon compounds are the raw materials that make up gas and oil. Once the gas and oil have formed into large pockets underground, they can then be extracted.

THE CLUE OF THE SALT DOMES

Oil traps are usually found where the rocks are buckled upwards in curved structures. The oil can gather beneath, like air in an upturned cup in a sinkful of water. The crumpled oil-bearing rocks of the Arabian Gulf have many traps, including those formed by "salt domes."

Since layers of salt are lighter than other rocks, they tend to rise through other rock layers, twisting them up as they go. The twisted beds form ideal traps, and it is structures like this that oil geologists look for.

Gas

Oil

Permeable rock

Impermeable rock

Water

A TYPICAL OIL TRAP

IRAQ

KUWAIT

SAUDI ARABIA

ZAGROS MOUNTAINS

IRAN

Main concentrations of oil

GAS AND PETROL IN THE NORTH SEA

The North Sea, between Great Britain and Europe, contains many oil traps.

Gas deposits are exploited in the southern North Sea, but these are derived from the break-down of coal deposits, not from oil.

NORTH SEA

Main gas production areas

Main gas pipelines

Left:
Because of the depth and fierce currents of the North Sea, the construction of gas and oil platforms has been highly developed.

Earth in action

The Earth changes before our eyes – water carves out channels through and under the ground, deserts sands shift in the wind...

Rivers

See also:
- **...lakes** p40
- **...and deltas** p42
- **Eroding earth** p44
- **Changing coasts** p62

Below:
Rivers can modify the land-scape through the processes of erosion and deposition. Typically, a river goes through three stages – the first is erosion, the third is deposition, and the second is a balance between the two, as shown by the photographs.

RIVERS ARE AN ESSENTIAL part of the water cycle on Earth. The sun evaporates water from the surfaces of the oceans. This water vapor is then blown over the continents by the winds.

When the atmosphere changes in pressure or in temperature, the water vapor condenses into clouds and falls as rain or snow. The water falling on the land eventually runs together to produce rivers that carry it back to the oceans once more. These cycles continue every second of every day and have done so for millions of years.

FIRST STAGE

SECOND STAGE

RIVER VALLEY
After passing through its first stage, the energy of the river is reduced. It can still erode a valley, but most erosion takes place at the sides, and the valley tends to be broad. This is the Shenandoah River in Virginia.

MOUNTAIN STREAM
A quickly flowing stream in the Alps is full of energy as it rushes down the mountainside, eroding its bed into a deep ravine. The eroded rock is picked up and carried along, adding to the erosive force.

FLOOD PLAIN
Eroded material begins to fall to the river bed as the current slackens, and soil and mud are laid on the valley floor. When it floods, whole sheets of sediment are deposited, giving a flat-bottomed valley which the river meanders over.

RIVER STAGES AND SHAPES

In the river's first stage, where it runs in a deep, V-shaped gorge, there is no depositing of material, only erosion.

In the second stage, where the river runs across layers of its own sediment, it is deeper on the outside curves, where the current is faster. It gradually erodes the outside of the curves and deposits sediment on the inside, so constantly changing its course.

In the third stage, so much sediment is deposited that the river may be above the level of the plain, held back by levees – banks of sediment deposited during floods.

FIRST STAGE PROFILE

SECOND STAGE PROFILE

THIRD STAGE PROFILE

THIRD STAGE

SPENT POWER
In the last stage of its life the river has lost most of its power. It slowly meanders across the land in great loops, often cut off as oxbow lakes. Mud and silt are deposited on the flood plain or near the river's mouth, as here on the coastal plain of Sarawak.

...lakes

See also:
- **Volcano!** p20
- **Spreading rifts** p22
- **Rivers** p38
- **...and delta** p42

Below:
Lakes form in the hollows gouged out by the weight of passing glaciers. Glaciers can also deposit rocky material (moraine), forming dams that hold back the water from the melting ice. The Great Lakes of North America are examples of huge glacier lakes.

THERE ARE THREE main kinds of lake: lakes scooped out by glaciers; lakes formed in hollows produced by the movements of the Earth, such as the Rift Valley lakes; and lakes formed where rivers flow into an inland basin. There are also artificial lakes, formed when a river is dammed, or when lagoons are cut off from the sea. Most lakes are fresh water, but some may accumulate minerals and become saltier than the sea. There are probably more lakes on the Earth's surface now than at any time in its history.

THE PRESENT DAY

Today the Chicago River flows into Lake Michigan, rather than out of it as it did 11,000 years ago.
 If the continent of North America continues to tilt it may flow out again in 1,500 years' time.

Below:
Over time the margins of lakes become overgrown with vege-tation. This gradually encroaches on the water until the lake becomes a swamp, and even covered over entirely.

Lake Erie was once the most polluted body of water in the world, because of industrial effluent flowing into it. Now with strict environmental controls the water is clear once more.

11,000 YEARS AGO
The eroded hollows filled with water as the ice began to melt. The water from the original Lake Michigan flowed southward to the Mississippi.

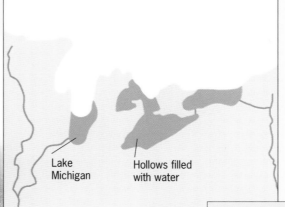

Lake Michigan

Hollows filled with water

11,000 YEARS AGO

LAKES FROM EARTH MOVEMENTS

Lake Baikal in Siberia is a typical rift valley lake. The rift valley was formed by plate movements that are slowly tearing Asia apart. As the valley has formed over the last 50 million years it has filled up with water, making it the oldest lake on Earth.

Other earth movement lakes include the crater lakes of extinct volcanoes, where the empty cone fills up with water. Crater Lake in Oregon is a good example, as are the *maars* of the Eifel district in Germany.

HOW THE LAKES BECAME GREAT

t the height of the last Ice Age half of North America was covred with ice. The ice sheet advanced southwards, scouring the urface and carrying along rubble and debris embedded in the e. When the ice melted at the end of the Ice Age, the hollows ft behind were filled with water and so became the Great akes. At certain times in the past the Great Lakes were much ore extensive than they are at present, shown by the presence f raised beaches. These lakes are estimated to contain about 20 ercent of the world's fresh water.

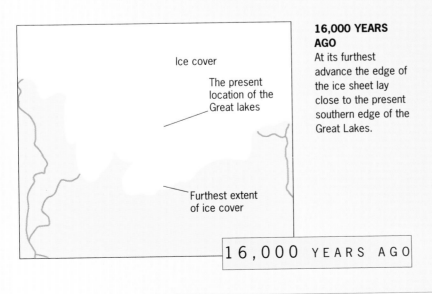

Ice cover

The present location of the Great lakes

Furthest extent of ice cover

16,000 YEARS AGO
At its furthest advance the edge of the ice sheet lay close to the present southern edge of the Great Lakes.

16,000 YEARS AGO

AUSTRALIA'S GREAT SALT LAKE

In desert areas the rivers from surrounding hills may flow into inland basins and form a lake in the wet season.

In the dry season the water all evaporates away, leaving plains of salt. This example is Lake Eyre in Southern Australia. Others exist in Death Valley, California.

...and deltas

See also:
- **Rivers** p38
- **...lakes** p40
- **Eroding earth** p44
- **Changing coasts** p62

Below:
The great sprawling mass of green in the desert shows the Okavango delta at the edge of the Kalahari Desert basin.
Most deltas are formed at the mouth of a river where it flows into the sea. This is a rare example of an inland delta, built up during the rainy seasons.

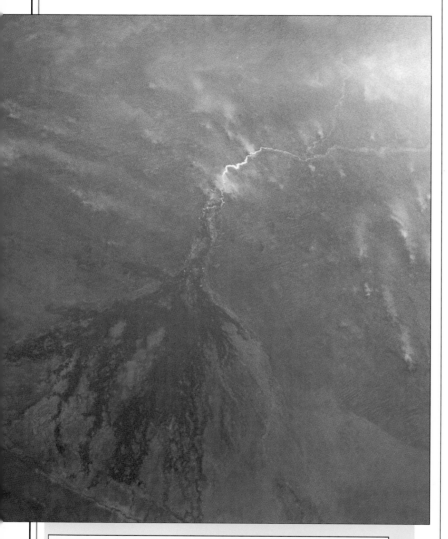

As a river flows into the sea it brings with it much of the sand and silt that it has picked up on its journey. If there are no strong tides or currents to wash it away, this sediment sinks to the bottom, building up gradually into sandbanks.

The river then gradually changes its course to find a way through, and may split up into many shifting channels. The result is a delta. The name was first given by the Ancient Greeks to the mouth of the Nile, which is shaped like the Greek letter Δ.

Deltas are very fertile, because of the rich silt, and have always attracted human settlement. Cairo, New Orleans, and Calcutta are all built on deltas.

THE MAKING OF THE NILE DELTA

Five and a half million years ago the Mediterranean Sea did not exist. The River Nile flowed from Africa on to a low desert plain which lay between North Africa and Europe. Over time the river laid down a huge alluvial "fan" of sediment. Today, most of the eastern Mediterranean is floored with this sediment.

The fertile silt, along with the constant water supply, mean that the Nile delta has been cultivated throughout history. However, its character is changing. The number of irrigation ditches in the delta has increased, and the flow of the Nile is now controlled by the Aswan Dam, starving the delta of new sediment. As a result, the front of the delta is now being eroded away.

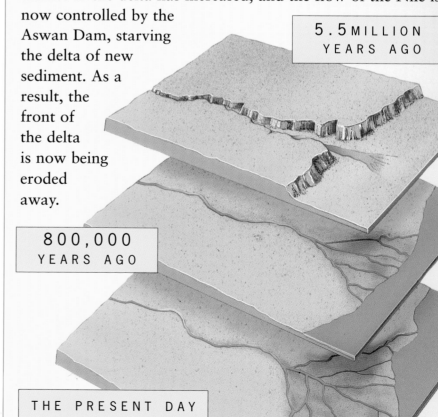

5.5 MILLION YEARS AGO

800,000 YEARS AGO

THE PRESENT DAY

THE INLAND DELTA

In Botswana, southern Africa, the Okavango River forms an inland delta as it spreads out at the edge of the vast semi-arid Kalahari Desert. Its seasonal watery fingers stretch out over 805 square miles.

In the rainy season water flows down to this delta and plant life flourishes. Grazing animals migrate there to feed as a relief from the dry conditions in the desert plains round about.

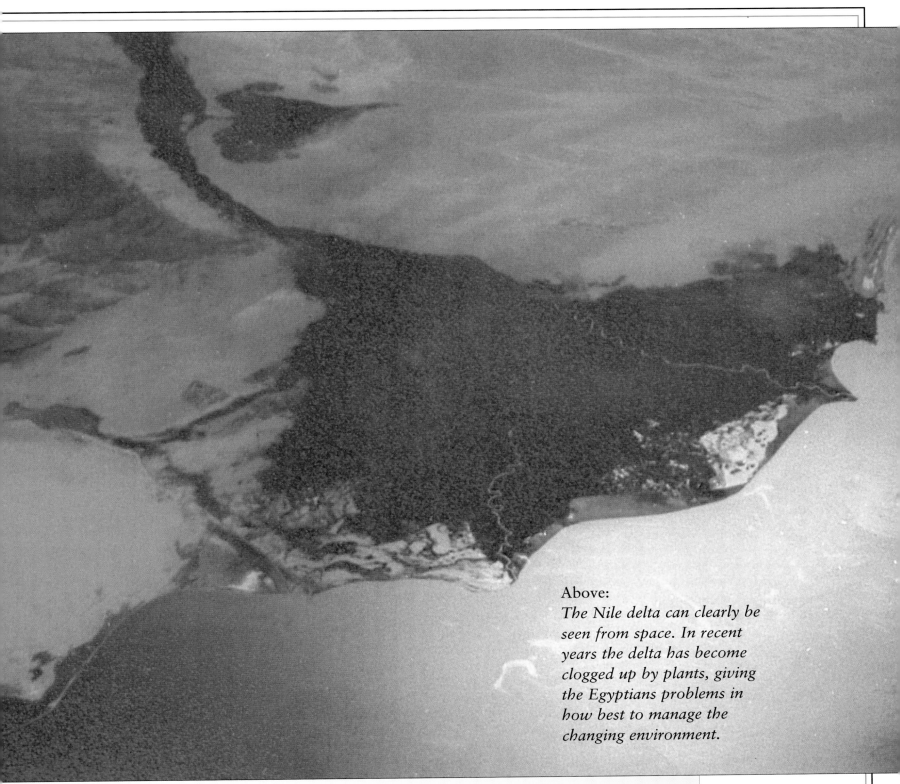

Above:
The Nile delta can clearly be seen from space. In recent years the delta has become clogged up by plants, giving the Egyptians problems in how best to manage the changing environment.

RIVER AND MAN

The Mississippi delta is what is known as a "bird's foot" delta. Its pattern is formed by the river channels forming levees (high banks of sediment) which reach out into the waters of the Gulf of Mexico.

The fact that the floor of the Gulf of Mexico is subsiding means that much of the sediment carried out to sea is spreading out on the sea floor, and the levees are left to form the delta.

The river today exits eastward, via New Orleans. But if man had not intervened to maintain the existing channels, it would have swung south again by now.

Eroding earth

See also:
- **Volcano!** *p20*
- **Spreading rifts** *p22*
- **Rivers** *p38*
- **...and deltas** *p42*

Below:
The Dalmatian coastline in Slovenia consists of islands and inlets running parallel to the shore, formed by the eroded ridges and valleys of parallel mountain ranges. The rocks are limestone, which have gradually been eroded and dissolved by water.

As SOON AS ROCKS are lifted above sea level the forces of nature combine to wear them away in a process known as erosion.

Physical erosion takes place when the sheer forces of the elements – wind, rain, ice, or sea waves – act on the rock to break it up and carry off the fragments.

In chemical erosion there is a chemical reaction between the minerals contained in the rocks and the atmosphere, causing the rocks to crumble and collapse.

FORCES AT WORK

A TYPICAL CAVE SYSTEM

Stalactite

Sink hole

Underground chamber

Stalagmite

Waterfall

Limestone is a porous rock which is very vulnerable to chemical weathering. Its main component is calcite, which is broken down by the acid in rainwater into calcium carbonate which then dissolves in the water.

The end result is a "karst" landscape, named for a region in Slovenia, where the barren limestone is dissolved into hollows and cracks, and the rocks beneath are riddled with potholes, caves, and caverns carved out by the water.

SPECTACULAR EFFECTS

A limestone cavern is shaped as the limestone is dissolved by the acid in rainwater. Horizontal galleries form along the water table and can be left dry if the water table drops. Side caves are eroded along joints and bedding planes in the rock where it is most vulnerable.

Right:
Water passing through limestone can build as well as destroy. The dissolved calcite in groundwater can be deposited on the walls and roofs of caves, giving spectacular stalagmites growing up, and stalactites coming down.

LANDSLIDES AND WATER

The most dramatic form of physical erosion is through landslides. These occur when a slope becomes unstable and can happen in several ways.

Very often it is human activities that trigger landslides. A landslide in Naples in 1998 happened because there was no control on building, and so too many houses were built on a slope that was not strong enough to take them.

In some areas the soil on a slope becomes unstable when vegetation is removed, and particularly when trees are felled. Rainwater then gradually moistens and loosens the soil until eventually a mass of mud slides downhill, often with disastrous results.

SOIL CREEP This is slow erosion through the gradual movement of soil and other particles downhill.

MUDSLIDES These occur on a slope when trees are felled and loose soil is then mixed with water during a storm.

SCREE This is a rubbly slope of broken rocks, split away from a hillside through the action of frost.

CLIFF SLUMPS. A mass of solid rock cracks and slides downward along a curved surface.

Shifting deserts

See also:
- **Polar regions** *p48*
- **Frozen earth** *p52*
- **Moving bands** *p54*
- **El Niño** *p58*

KUISEB RIVER BOUNDARY
The Kuiseb River washes the creeping sand into the ocean. Coastal sand spits show the northward-flowing cold current that produces the typical coastal desert conditions.

THE GREAT SAND SEA
The pattern of dunes in the Namib Desert shows how the prevailing winds are constantly moving the sand northward.

Above:
The sheer size and intense color of the great Namib Desert makes it easy to distinguish from the Space Shuttle.

The three different kinds of desert are all to be found within its boundaries.

DESERTS OCCUR where there is very little rainfall – usually less than 10in per year, falling in one brief season. Most deserts are hot, but some can be found in cold areas, such as the Taklamakan Desert in China. They can also be found on the tops of high plateaus where there is little rainfall.

The popular image of a desert as a place where nothing grows is actually quite rare. Desert vegetation can consist of very poor grassland or scrub, and succulent plants such as cacti.

SKELETON COAST

The Namib is a coastal desert, formed by the cold sea currents flowing from the Antarctic. The cold sea cools the air above and causes it to descend. As rain only falls from ascending air, this produces dry desert conditions.

Toward the east, the Namib Desert shades into the Kalahari, a tropical desert. Warm air rises at the Equator, dropping all its moisture as rain and producing rainforest. As this dry air drifts away from the Equator it cools and descends at the latitude of the Tropics, producing the tropical desert belts.

DESERT ZONES

Tropical deserts form along the Tropics, where dry air descends. These include the Sahara and Mexican deserts along the Tropic of Cancer, and the Kalahari and Australian deserts along the Tropic of Capricorn.

Continental deserts, such as the Gobi, are dry because of their distance from the sea. Coastal deserts such as the Atacama and the Namib form where cold ocean currents flow towards the Equator.

Rain shadow deserts, such as those in California and Patagonia, lie in the lee of mountains where only dry air reaches them.

Key

▢	Tropical
▢	Continental
▢	Rain shadow
▢	Cold

ROCKY AND STONY DESERTS
The Namib Desert is an example of the three kinds of desert.

It not only has sand, but also contains stretches of stony desert pavement and exposed bedrock with little soil.

THREE KINDS OF DESERT

Within the various desert zones there are three different types of desert, each producing its own distinctive land forms.

Wind is the most powerful agent in the formation of desert landscapes.

SAND DESERT
The sand sea is the most familiar desert type. Wind erosion reduces exposed rocks to sand, blown along in slow waves called dunes.

STONY DESERT
The stony desert, or pavement, is a surface of wind-polished stones. This may be only a surface crust, sealing off a layer of finer dust

ROCKY DESERT
Dry desert conditions mean that few plants grow, and no soil can form. The bedrock of the landscape is exposed and eroded.

THE DESERT AREAS OF THE WORLD

60°N
Turkmenistan
Gobi
Mojave
Iran
Chihuahua
Taklamakan   30°N
Thar
Sahara   Arabia
Somalia
Equator
Atacama
Australian deserts
Namib
30°S
Kalahari
Monte
Patagonia
60°S
Antarctica

Polar regions

See also:
- **Volcano!** *p20*
- **Spreading rifts** *p22*
- **Rivers of ice** *p50*
- **Holes in the sky** *p76*

Left and right:
The two great masses of Antarctica (right) *and the Arctic* (below) *are shown here on satellite images. The Arctic is mainly frozen sea. Antarctica is a land mass covered by an ice sheet.*

THE TWO GREAT MASSES of ice at either end of the planet hold well over 90 per cent of the world's fresh water supply. Each year as the globe gets warmer, the ice shrinks and the oceans get deeper. In Antarctica, the average thickness of the ice is 6,500ft. In the Arctic the sea ice is 10 to 16ft thick.

There are no volcanoes in the Arctic, but five active ones have been found in Antarctica.

Below:
Arctic icebergs floats away into the North Atlantic Ocean. These icebergs are sharply shaped, unlike their flat-topped Antarctic cousins.

FIVE VARIETIES OF ICE

FRAZIL ICE

GREASE ICE

PANCAKE ICE

SEA-ICE SHEETS

ICE-FLOES

Scientists have recognized five different forms of ice in the polar regions. The Arctic has a more placid sea and only four of the five types (not frazil ice) are found there.

Frazil ice
Water that freezes fast, causing chaotic crystal growth, shows evidence of stormy seas

AN ICY SLIVER

In Antarctic ice, two distinct layers can be found, unlike Arctic ice where it is usual to find only one. This base layer, called congelation ice, is associated with calm, still waters.

Congelation ice

As icebergs 'calve' off ice shelves, they can break away in a spectacular manner – this iceberg (below) photographed from 352 miles high, was larger than the state of Rhode Island (1,949 square miles).

ALPHA 24, SOUTH ATLANTIC

The visible size of an iceberg is deceptive, as over two thirds of it lie under the water. Perhaps the most famous iceberg was the one that the *Titanic* hit in 1912; over 1,500 died.

ICEBERGS IN THE MAKING

Roald Amundsen, the Norwegian polar explorer, once camped on the Ross Ice Shelf of Antarctica. He thought this was firm ground, but in recent years the shelf has been breaking up. Some experts attribute this to pressure caused by a fault deep under the landmass.

THE SHELF AT REST
This series of images, taken over a period of three years from a US defence satellite, shows the gradual disintegration of the Ross Ice Shelf on the Antarctic continent.

NOVEMBER 1986

CRACKS APPEAR
Almost a year after the first picture was taken, a long diagonal crack appears at the seaward edge of the shelf.
A second crack immediately below also shows signs of breaking away.

OCTOBER 1987

BREAKAWAY
A large chunk of ice has broken free and floated away, drifting into the middle of the image. Snowfalls have covered the secondary crack, which is now showing signs of lengthening before it too breaks free of the main ice mass.

DECEMBER 1988

Rivers of ice

See also:
- **Building mountains** *p24*
- **Polar regions** *p48*
- **Lakes** *p40*
- **Changing coasts** *p62*

Below:
This image from a Landsat satellite shows part of the Byrd Glacier in Antarctica. The ice flow can be seen oozing out between the mountain ranges, together with the dark streaks of moraine (rocky debris).

GLACIERS ARE "the ploughs of the Earth." The raw power that they harness rips up the land beneath and crumbles it into powdered rock. Glaciers shape the earth over which they move by carving out huge valleys over millions of years. They can transport rock boulders weighing hundreds of tons and then deposit them, as the glacier slowly melts, many miles away. Although glaciers are so powerful most move less than 3ft in a year.

These rivers of ice can be a thousand feet wide and many miles long. They cover almost 11 percent of the world's land surface.

WHERE TO FIND ICE

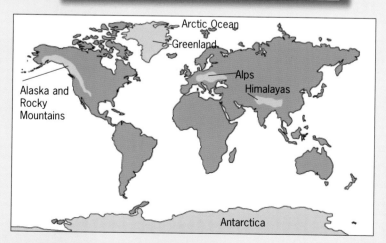

Arctic Ocean
Greenland
Alps
Himalayas
Alaska and Rocky Mountains
Antarctica

Over 6 million square miles of the Earth are permanently covered with ice. This includes the Arctic sea ice, the huge Antarctic and Greenland ice sheets, ice caps, ice shelves, and high altitude glaciers.

THE ANATOMY OF A GLACIER

now gathers in a hollow – cirque – at the top of a
mountain. As the snow builds up, it spills over and
lowly flows down like a river. Crevasses, or cracks,
orm where the the angle of the slope changes. Rocky
ebris – moraine – is left at the sides and at the foot.

Cirque

Lateral moraine

Terminal moraine

Crevasse

Above:
*A sinister puff of snow
that can signal death and
destruction in a few
fleeting moments.*

Left:
*The Cook Glacier in
New Zealand's South
Island shows many of its
classic glacial landscape
features from space.*

AVALANCHE!

In a moment a puff of snow and a
distant rumble can herald the onset
of an avalanche.

One of the worst avalanches of
recent years occurred in Peru in
1962 when 3 million tons of debris
from the glacial ice mass above Mt
Huascaran fell onto the slope of the
main glacier and cascaded down
onto the villages in the valley below.
This avalanche of rock, ice, and
mud, already about 45 ft high,
gathered more debris as it descend-
ed down the valley. When its
journey ended 2 minutes later 2,400
people were dead.

Frozen earth

See also:
- **Polar regions** p48
- **Rivers of ice** p50
- **Moving bands** p54

IN THE NORTHERN hemisphere, the last vegetation zone after the tree line and before the ice cap is known as tundra. In the southern hemisphere only the southern tip of South America has tundra – Antarctica is almost totally covered in ice.

These northern plains are covered with snow and ice in the winter. In the short summer the ice and snow melts, but the water cannot drain away, and so great areas of lake, pond, and marsh develop in the tundra areas of Alaska, Canada, and Siberia.

Above and right:
Two views of the Canadian tundra taken from a Landsat orbiter in false color (above) and from the Space Shuttle (right). The bleakness of these wastes is well conveyed in these true color images.

Below:
The great landmass of Asia in summer, showing the tundra regions. Reindeer and musk ox find enough to eat in the mosses, grasses, and lichens in the summer, but migrate south to the forests in the winter.

Above:
Repeated freezing and thawing breaks the topsoil into polygons, as shown here at Spitzbergen.

ICE POWER

There is a permanently frozen layer of ice in the soil at these latitudes. In Siberia and Canada the permafrost can be as deep as 1,650ft. It remains frozen even in summer when the surface soil thaws out. This means that the meltwater cannot drain away.

Repeated freezing and thawing of the top layer of soil creates patterns of stones on the surface – polygons – and low hills, known as pingoes. Pingoes are mounds of ice which are constantly enlarging from below, stressing and cracking the crust of soil on the top.

PERMAFROST SLICE

Soil thaws in the summer

Permafrost – permanently frozen soil

BOUNDARIES IN ICE

There are no tall trees in the tundra, where the ground is frozen for most of the year, because it has a very short growing season. Mosses, lichens, and grasses are the only vegetation that appears in the summer. The few trees that survive are stunted, as they cannot grow in the long, dark winter with its icy winds. As the tundra nears the polar region, the trees disappear altogether.

Limit of tree line around the North polar region

Right:
Tombstone Valley in the Yukon, Alaska, is set alight by autumn color. For a few short weeks the low scrub, plants and lichen transform the tundra wilderness into a blaze of technicolor tints.

Moving bands

See also:
- ...lakes *p40*
- ...and deltas *p42*
- **Shifting deserts** *p46*

Above:
A composite image of the Earth showing how vegetation and habitats form a mirror image north and south of the Equator.

THE NATURAL VEGETATION ZONES of the Earth closely follow the climate zones, because plant life is very much controlled by climate. Hot and wet conditions, as along the Equator, produce forest. In seasonal dry conditions grasses and grassy plains thrive, but not trees. In dry climates only desert vegetation is found. Very cold climates produce forests of conifers – trees that can withstand freezing conditions and shake off heavy coverings of snow.

WHY THERE ARE SEASONS

The Earth's axis is tilted at an angle to its orbit around the sun, so at one time of year the North Pole is pointing towards the sun, and six months later it is pointing away. While the North Pole is pointing towards the sun, the northern hemisphere absorbs more sunlight – it is summer in the north and winter in the south. Six months later the situation is reversed.

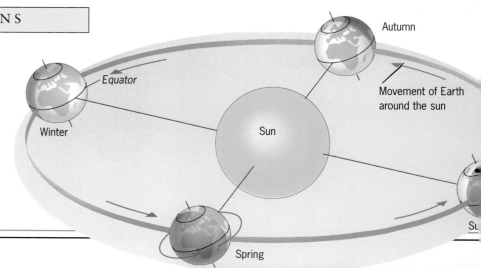

Autumn

Equator

Movement of Earth around the sun

Winter

Sun

Spring

Su

SUN AND RAIN

The main factors that affect climate, and so vegetation, are temperature and humidity.

The climate in the various parts of the world is determined by how much sunlight they receive, and how much rain falls, at what time of the year.

The distance from the Equator is a factor in this, as is the position in relation to the prevailing winds that may or may not bring moisture from the oceans.

The colors in the diagram represent the many kinds of climate in the world. Even though they look complex and inter-linked, the same broad bands of vegetation reflect each other north and south of the Equator.

New York London Omsk Singapore

Rainfall

Temperature

CLIMATE ZONES

Rainfall

Temperature

Manaus   Alice Springs   Lagos

Right:
The charts in this diagram show typical sun and rain-fall temperatures through-out the world.

TEMPERATE TAKEOVER

No open land will remain barren for long if it is possible for plants to grow. At the end of the last Ice Age, about 10,000 years ago, the land left by the retreating glaciers was quickly colonized by vegetation.

First to come were small plants such as mosses and lichens, which started to create a soil. Then came tough grasses and heathers. The first trees were small, hardy types such as birch and rowan, followed by conifers. Then, as the climate improved, deciduous forest was established.

Barren land   Small plants and grass   Scrub land and coarse grasses   Coniferous woodland   Deciduous woodland

Ocean currents

See also:
- **Rivers** *p38*
- **...and deltas** *p42*
- **Seas and tides** *p60*
- **Changing coasts** *p62*

MORE THAN TWO-THIRDS of the surface of the Earth is covered with water, and this water is in constant motion. Surface currents are driven by the winds, while the deep currents are driven by the circulation of warm and cold water, and by the Coriolis effect. These powerful currents move water across entire oceans, bringing warm weather to cold coastal areas, and cooling regions that would otherwise be hot.

MEDDIES
Every time the tide goes in and out of the Mediterranean it surges between the Straits of Gibraltar, creating pulses of water with a different salinity from the Atlantic Ocean where they exit. These pulses are known as "Meddies."

ICEBERG CARRIERS
The coast off Labrador has a cold southerly ocean current that brings with it drifting icebergs, calved off from Greenland and the neighboring Labrador Coast. Over 700 icebergs move south on this current each year, some travelling many hundreds of miles.

This page:
The ocean can provide many surprising images, a these pictures show. The different currents and depths of the water can show as distinct patterns even on hand held satellite images, helping oceanographers to plot the movements of these vast bodies of water.

PACIFIC SWIRL
This mass of swirling water, glinting in the sun in the Sea of Japan, is many hundreds of miles wide and forms part of a gyre. It is formed by the meeting of the Kuroshia, Oyashio and North Pacific Currents.

OCEAN CORKSCREWS

The surface currents of the oceans are controlled by the global wind pattern. The main ocean current is called a gyre. These currents sweep around the ocean basins, moving clockwise in the northern hemisphere, and counterclockwise in the southern hemisphere.

The various "legs" of a gyre produce warm currents along the western sides of the oceans and cold currents along the eastern sides.

In the North Atlantic the western current is the Gulf Stream, which brings warm water across the Atlantic from the West Indies to northern Europe.

SHIFTING SANDS

Ocean currents have a strong influence on the shape of the coastline. When currents move in one prevailing direction they constantly move the sand along the shoreline in that direction.

In this way sand bars are gradually built out from the land in gentle sweeps and curves. When the current sweeps past a bay, then the sand bar curves back in a sort of hook as eddies swirl around the tip. The bar is a constantly shifting piece of land. England's Spurn Point has rebuilt itself some six or seven times over the course of the last two hundred years.

Below:
Cape Cod in Massachusetts is a sand spit with a characteristic curve at the tip. It is one of many spits produced by the North Atlantic Drift.

 Hot currents   Cold currents

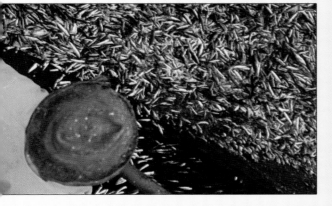

Above:
The cold deep ocean currents, such as those in the North Atlantic and the Eastern Pacific, are rich in nutrients, and so support vast shoals of fish.

El Niño

See also:
- **Ocean currents** p56
- **Global weather** p68
- **Clouds and storms** p70

17 MARCH 1997

FIRST WAVE
The progress of the 1997–8 El Niño was charted by false-color photographs taken by the US National Oceano-graphic and Atmospheric Administration satellite.

THE NORTH-EAST AND SOUTH-EAST trade winds in the Pacific combine to drive the warm surface water westward. Every few years, however, these waters change direction and flow eastward instead. This change in the ocean circulation, because of a change in the winds, has side-effects on the climate all over the globe. The effect is known El Niño, or the child, because it often happens around Christmas.

MAKING WAVES

In the past, an El Niño event occurred once in ten years or so. The trade winds changed direction from west to east and the warm surface waters accumulated in the west begin to move eastwards, pooling in the east Pacific and beginning El Niño. This unaccustomed warm water in the eastern Pacific prevented the usual rise of cold water from the deep trenches of the ocean bed. In the 1990s El Niño has became so frequent and long-lasting that it has almost become the norm, and is likely to have long-lasting effects on world climate.

21 MARCH 1997

BUILD-UP
The first photograph above (17 March) shows the warm water (shown in red and white) in the Equatorial west Pacific. Four days later the warm water was beginning to reach eastward.

Above:
Even as far away as Africa "El Niño" has upset the continent's balance of sun and rain.

EVENT HORIZON
A month later the warm water had reached the coast of South America, bring-ing unseasonal warm conditions to the Galapagos Islands and to Peru which suffered flooding and violent storms. It also destroyed the Peruvian anchovy harvest.

ALTERING CLIMATE

The effects of El Niño are felt much further afield than the eastern Pacific. Land areas in the western Pacific are prone to typhoons, like the one which killed 6,000 in the Philippines in 1991. Australia, Africa, and South-east Asia suffer from droughts, causing poor harvests. The tinder dry conditions also contribute to the disastrous fires in the rainforests of Sumatra and Borneo which have destroyed wildlife and caused widespread pollution.

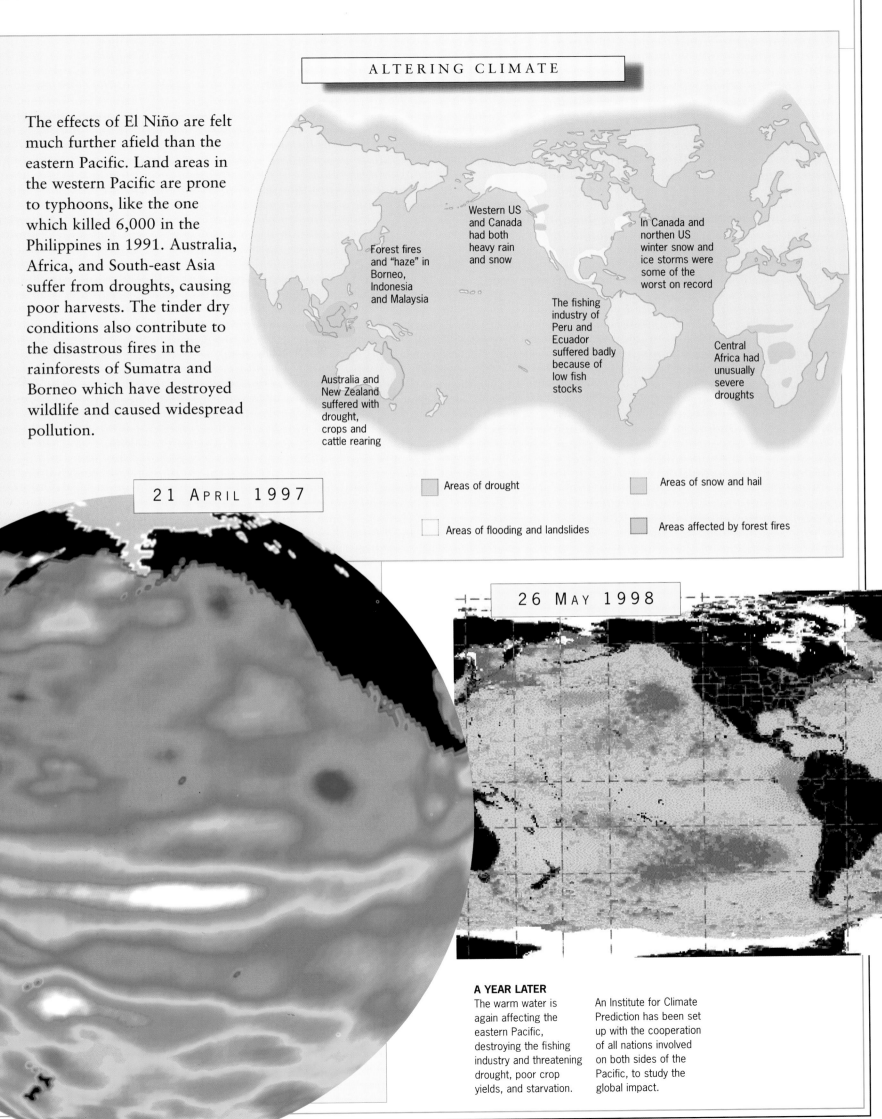

Forest fires and "haze" in Borneo, Indonesia and Malaysia

Western US and Canada had both heavy rain and snow

In Canada and northen US winter snow and ice storms were some of the worst on record

The fishing industry of Peru and Ecuador suffered badly because of low fish stocks

Central Africa had unusually severe droughts

Australia and New Zealand suffered with drought, crops and cattle rearing

21 APRIL 1997

Areas of drought

Areas of snow and hail

Areas of flooding and landslides

Areas affected by forest fires

26 MAY 1998

A YEAR LATER
The warm water is again affecting the eastern Pacific, destroying the fishing industry and threatening drought, poor crop yields, and starvation.

An Institute for Climate Prediction has been set up with the cooperation of all nations involved on both sides of the Pacific, to study the global impact.

Seas and tides

See also:
- **Changing coasts** p62
- **Global weather** p68
- **Clouds and Storms** p70

DEEP BLUE HOLES

The ocean can be divided into depth zones. Closest to land is the continental shelf, the flooded edges of the continent. This is only 450ft or so at its deepest, although the Tongue of the Ocean, in the Bahamas (*below*) is over one mile deep. Beyond this the continental slope drops away into the abyssal plain, the true ocean floor, with an average depth of 12,000ft. Some oceans have deep trenches. The deepest is the Mindanao Trench in the western Pacific, which is over 36,000ft deep.

VISIT A SEASHORE and you will see constant change. Twice a day tides gradually creep up the beach and then slowly retreat again.

Over a month (28 days), the tides alternate between the strong spring tides and the weaker neap tides, depending on the alignment of the sun, moon, and Earth.

Waves are created when the wind blows over the water surface, piling it up into ridges which then move in the direction of the wind, big waves during storms and small ripples in calm weather.

BREAKERS ON THE SHORE

Direction of wind and waves

Wave breaks on shore

Circular motion of energy

Waves spread out

Waves tightly packed together

ATTACKING WAVES
Waves expend their energy travelling forward and back in a circular motion. Their strength depends on the shape of the coast and the depth of the water.

WAVE ACTION

Winds passing over the surface of the ocean whip it up into waves, the water particles blasted forward and back in a circular motion. Although the water itself is only moving with this limited action, the wave disturbance can travel thousands of miles.

On reaching shallow water the circular motion drags on the bottom and the wave topples over to form a breaker. When wave fronts approach land they tend to curve around exposed headlands, attacking their cliffs from either side.

HIGH RISE AND FALL

The shape of the shoreline has an effect on the tides. The highest tidal range occurs where there are long bays and inlets, forcing the rising water into narrow gaps.

The Bay of Fundy, in Canada, (*see right*) has a tidal range of 44ft at the strong spring tides, when the Sun and Moon are exerting a pull together.

MOON POWER

The Earth and Moon swing round each other, causing bulges of water (tides) dragged toward the Moon on one side of the Earth, and thrown away from it on the other. In this diagram the swing of the Moon has been exaggerated. The harbor (see diagram) is marked x.

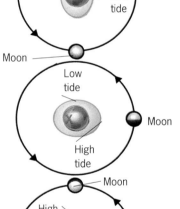

Moon

High tide

Low tide

High tide

Low tide

Moon

Low tide

High tide

Moon

Moon

High tide

Low tide

1 SEPTEMBER
High tide at harbor x, because the Moon directly overhead is pulling the water that way.

8 SEPTEMBER
Harbor x now has a low tide because the Moon has gone 90° around the Earth.

15 SEPTEMBER
Harbor x has a high tide again, because a water bulge is being created by the Earth's swing around the Moon.

22 SEPTEMBER
Low tide again at harbor x because it is midway between the tidal bulges once more.

Changing coasts

See also:
- **Eroding earth** *p44*
- **Ocean currents** *p56*
- **Seas and tides** *p60*

Below:
A Landsat compositional mosaic of the British Isles shows many examples of changing coastal scenery. Since the end of the Ice Age the region has been gradually tilting, with northern Scotland rising out of the water, and southern England slowly submerging.

RISING LAND
Around much of Scotland the coastline shows raised beaches – shelves of sand tens of feet above the present-day beach. These represent the level of the beaches during the Ice Age.

SCOTTISH FJORDS
On the West Coast of Scotland 400 million-year-old mountains are being attacked by the rough seas of the Atlantic, producing the typical eroded coastline of sea lochs and peninsulas.

SOUTH-WEST BRITAIN
The estuaries of Devon and Cornwall are flooded river valleys, submerged over the last few thousand years.

THE BOUNDARY between the land and sea is constantly changing. In some areas the land is slowly being pounded and worn away by the action of the sea; elsewhere the sea deposits sand and shingle along the shore, gradually changing the coastline.

This results in two types of coastline. An eroded coast is admired for its rugged grandeur, as with the Scottish West Coast, while a coast where material is deposited provides the holidaymaker with sandy beaches.

HARD ROCKS, SOFT ROCKS

Mountain ranges jutting out into the sea are constantly broken down and eroded by the perpetual pounding of the waves. Such a coastline is jagged, with many headlands and inlets.

The material broken away from the land on an eroded coast often ends up on another coast which is slowly being built up. The broken rocky material from one area is slowly reduced to sand and shingle by the action of the sea. It is then spread by the action of the waves along beaches where the land is flatter. From the sky, a coastline that is gradually being built up has a smooth margin, often swept into spits and sand bars by the prevailing sea currents.

THE NORTH SEA
The North Sea rests on a low submerged continental shelf. It is crossed from north to south by shallow "stretch marks" which indicate a slowly expanding sea-bed.

FORCES AT WORK

Along a coast that is being built up, rather than eroded, the sand and shingle are constantly on the move. Waves strike the coast at an angle, and wash the sand in a diagonal path up the beach. Some of this sand is washed straight back down in the backwash, and the next wave washes it up again at an angle. In this way sand and shingle gather in a zigzag path along the beach. This process is known as beach drift, or longshore drift.

Swash

Direction of wind and waves

Backwash

BEACH MOVEMENT

BAY OF WHALES

When beach drift meets an inlet, the sand builds a sand bar across the mouth, forming a shallow lagoon. If it is across a river mouth, it will form a half-bar, or spit.

When beach drift reaches a headland, it builds the sand out into the sea as a spit. Sometimes the spit reaches as far as an island, and so joins the island to the mainland. This is called a tombolo. Jervis Bay in Australia is flanked by two tombolos.

Barrier Dike

Wienngen-meer 1927-30

Ijsselmeer

North East polder 1937-50

Markerwald (not yet reclaimed)

East Friesland 1950-57

AMSTERDAM

South Friesland 1959-68

WINDMILLS AND WATER

The Dutch have been altering their coastline since the 7th century. The shallow inlets of the Netherlands have been gradually walled off into "polders" and pumped out to provide farm land – 3,000 square miles in the past 800 years. The water in this land, some of it 15ft below sea level, has to be constantly drained, using ditches, canals, pumps, and the traditional windmills.

Coral islands

See also:
- **Volcano!** *p20*
- **Spreading rifts** *p22*
- **Rivers** *p38*
- **...and deltas** *p42*

RAIATEA
The single narrow fringing reef that surrounds both Raiatea and Tahaa can clearly be seen.

Below:

The Society Islands in French Polynesia display all the types of coral growth. They stretch from the south-east to the north-west, those in the south-east (top left) being the youngest.

CORALS ARE TINY ORGANISMS, ranging in size from one-tenth of an inch to several inches, which are found in shallow tropical seas. Corals live in large colonies, in limestone shells. As each one dies, a new one grows on top of its skeleton. In this way over thousands of years they construct huge masses of limestone, called reefs. The Great Barrier Reef, along the north-east coast of Australia, extends for 1,250 miles.

These reefs provide a haven for all kinds of marine wildlife. Unfortunately, corals are very delicate, and so are very vulnerable to the effects of tourism, commercial fishing, and environmental pollution.

BORA-BORA
This is a classic island with a barrier reef which is hundreds of thousands of years older than its two sister islands (left). It has a well-developed barrier reef on all sides as well as broad reef flats.

TAHAA
This island has subsided slightly more than her sister Raiatea and so has a barrier reef off-shore. Both islands have high volcanic valleys with steeply eroded and wooded sides that end in a thin strip of beach.

THE LIFE AND DEATH OF A CORAL ISLAND

When an island is formed by volcanic action, coral builds around the coast, building a fringing reef. Later the island may subside and become smaller as the sea floor subsides. The reef continues to grow upward, separated from the shrinking island by a lagoon, forming a barrier reef. When the island sinks completely, because the sea floor has subsided, the coral is left forming a ring-shaped reef called an atoll.

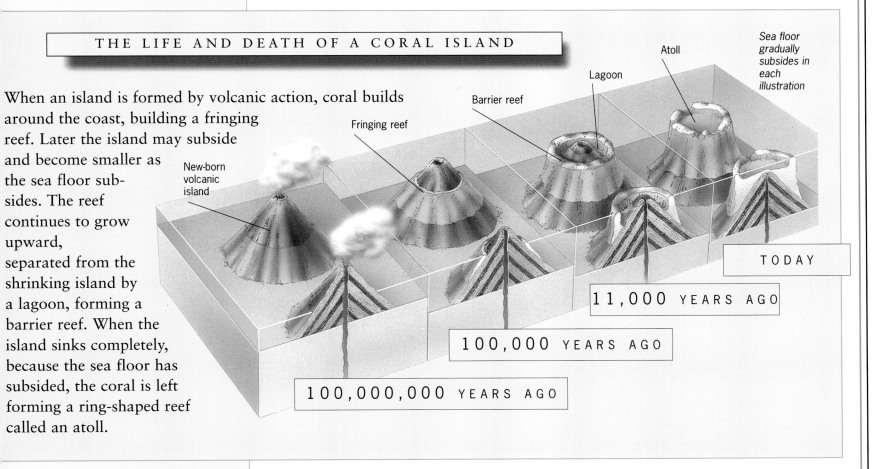

Sea floor gradually subsides in each illustration

Atoll

Lagoon

Barrier reef

Fringing reef

New-born volcanic island

TODAY

11,000 YEARS AGO

100,000 YEARS AGO

100,000,000 YEARS AGO

THE WORLDS BIGGEST ATOLL

Kiritimati is the largest atoll in the Pacific Ocean. Previously known as Christmas Island, it was discovered by Captain Cook on Christmas Eve in 1777.

Because of its remote position and barrenness, it was used as a testing site for nuclear weapons in the 1950s and 1960s.

TUPAI
This is the oldest of the islands shown. The central island has completely submerged, leaving a series of submerged reefs and lagoons, called an atoll. There are only three gaps in the reef.

Right:
A typical view of a Pacific coral island. The sea is shallow and exceptionally clear, with the reef growing only a few inches below the surface of the water.

PART THREE

Unseen forces

Under the sea, on land, and in the air hidden forces are slowly altering the balance of our living planet

Global weather

See also:
- **The air around us** *p14*
- **Ocean currents** *p56*
- **El Niño** *p58*
- **Clouds and storms** *p70*

FAST LANES IN THE SKY

High in the atmosphere there is a mysterious system of very fast winds. These are the so-called jet streams, a tube-like core of very fast winds which encircles the Earth. The jet stream is 100 miles wide and 2–5 miles deep, and the winds blow eastwards at speeds of up to 250 mph. East-bound airliners use these jet streams to save on time and fuel.

Cold air from Pole

Jet stream

Westerly winds

Below:
Over the Red Sea and the Nile in Egypt a satellite photograph picks up a jet stream as a swathe of clouds across the sky.

OUR WEATHER is the result of the movement of winds across the Earth. The energy from the sun produces the heat of the Equator. Hot air rises at the Equator, spreads north and south, then descends at about the latitude of the Tropics. From there, the warm air spreads out to the Poles, and also back to the Equator as surface winds. Cold air descends over the Poles and spreads outward. This movement of winds is not due north and due south because of the Coriolis effect (*see right*).

Cold air descending

Trade winds

Hot air rising

"...TURN, TURN"

As the Earth spins on its axis the Equator moves faster than anywhere else, because the Earth is widest there, and so has further to travel in 24 hours.

Anything – wind or an aeroplane – moving toward the Equator is travelling over land that is moving eastward faster and faster, and so it finds itself lagging behind – it is deflected to the west. Likewise anything that sets off due north from the Equator is deflected to the east. South of the Equator the reverse happens. This is called the Coriolis effect.

Rotation of the Earth

Actual path of trade winds

Equator

Theoretical path of trade winds

SWIRLING WIND
Surface winds over the Pacific Ocean. The arrows show what direction the winds are blowing.

Right:
Winds sucked into a depression move into a spiral pattern because of the Coriolis effect. Moving away from the Equator they are deflected eastward; moving towards the Equator they are deflected westward.

Clouds and storms :

See also:
The air around us *p14*   • **El Niño** *p58*
Ocean currents *p56*   • **Killer winds** *p72*

WATER, which is essential for life on Earth, exists in three forms. Depending on temperature and air pressure, water can exist as a liquid, as a solid (ice), or as gas (vapor).

Clouds are formed when water vapor in the air condenses into tiny droplets of water. In warm clouds, swirling air currents make the droplets collide and join together into larger droplets, which eventually fall as rain. These are the white fluffy cumulus clouds, or the low, gray stratus clouds.

If the cloud has a temperature below freezing, the water vapor turns into ice crystals. These high cirrus clouds look quite different – more feathery and wispy – from the fluffy cumulus.

THE PATTERNS IN THE SKY SHOW

Above and below:
Cloud patterns formed by wind show how, like water, wind flows around an obstruction.

In Western Australia clouds have formed over peaks of the Chichester range. These "pointed" clouds are rare.

We are all familiar with the appearance of clouds as seen from below – the dark underbelly of storm clouds or the high, wispy mare's tails that suggest a change of weather is on the way. They look even more spectacular from above, their shapes depending on whether there is land or sea below.

Left:
When wind blows over a flat hill crest, wave-like wind currents can build up clouds downwind, to the left of the obstacle. These cloud waves were photographed over South Australia.

THE SOUND AND LIGHT SHOW

Thunderclouds form in warm, rapidly rising moist air. As it rises, the moisture condenses, forming towering cumulonimbus clouds. Air circulation is so strong in these clouds that the raindrops cannot fall, but just become bigger and more unstable. Eventually, they break apart, releasing an electric charge. This electricity discharged to the ground forms a lighting flash, while the air expands with a crack of thunder.

Positive charge

Sheet lighting

Negative charge

Cumulonimbus clouds

Positive charge

Positive charge

Negative charge

Positive charge

Forked lightning

Above and right:
A tropical storm above Brazil shows off its icy "anvil" head while fork lightning hits the desert.

Killer winds

See also:
- **The air around us** *p14*
- **Ocean currents** *p56*
- **Global weather** *p68*
- **Clouds and storms** *p70*

25 AUG 1992 19:00HRS UTC
"ANDREW"APPROACHES LOUISIANA

Above and right:
In August 1992, hurricane Andrew caused the most damage and highest death toll of any hurricane in living memory. Between 23 August and 27 August, it had been responsible for 52 deaths and $22 billion in damage in the Bahamas, Louisiana and Florida. (see below).

26 AUG 1992 UTC
"ANDREW" HITS THE COAST

T HE TWO most powerful storms known to man are hurricanes and tornados. Both can wreak havoc on an almost unimaginable scale within seconds, and with little warning.

THE COILED SERPENT

Hurricanes are formed in hot climates, when are as of low atmospheric pressure form over tropical oceans.

Large amounts of moisture evaporate, and as the hot air rises more air is drawn in at sea level with great force. The wind spirals inward and upward counterclockwise around a central "eye" to produce the hurricane effect.

The Coriolis effect – the difference in the speed of rotation of the Earth close to and away from the Equator – is responsible for the spiral structure and the westward movement of the whole system.

HOW HURRICANES FORM

winds flowing outward

eye of storm

winds turn counter-clockwise

strong upcurrents

Low pressure over warm seas draws in air at sea level with great force. As this hot air rises it cause winds to spiral upwards counter-clockwise around the "eye" or center. Thick storm clouds form as the moisture condenses on the way up. At the top the dry, cooler air spreads outward.

The satellite picture shows the spiral of air spreading outward at height. Note the devastating winds spiralling inward counterclockwise at sea level.

"LET'S TWIST AGAIN..."

Tornados are formed when hot and cold air masses meet and shear past one another during a thunderstorm. This causes small areas of intense low pressure which bring air swirling inward counterclockwise in a narrow column to form the tornado.

The funnel-shaped cloud quickly extends to the ground and then swirls across land at immense speeds of more than 100mph. It destroys buildings, sucks up people and vehicles and flattens everything in its path.

Above and right:
Tornados seen over Texas from a weather satellite and from the ground.

WHERE THE WINDS CAN KILL
The map below shows the distribution of hurricanes and tornados. Those areas of intense storms are indicated in red; those areas where it is less likely are shaded pink.

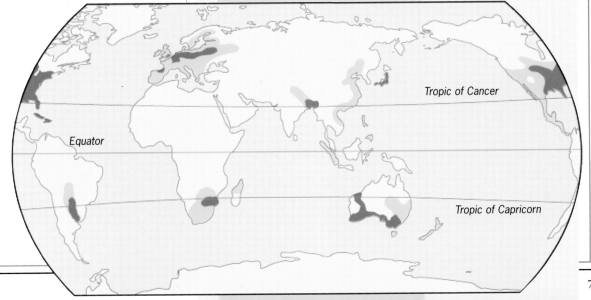

Tropic of Cancer

Equator

Tropic of Capricorn

Marks of man

See also:
- **Squashed forests** p32
- **Black gold** p34
- **Shifting deserts** p46
- **Moving bands** p54

M AN HAS PUT his impression on many parts of the Earth's surface. Some of it for good, some for more misguided reasons. The effects, whatever the cause, are plain to see, and from space are even more evident.

The Great Wall of China can be easily recognized from an orbiting spacecraft. Trackways can be traced in the desert, ruined cities plotted in rainforest mountains. The remote sensing equipment of satellites can shed light on an ancient past as easily as observing the progress of a modern war.

At night our planet shimmers with light, like fireflies hovering in the sky on a warm summer evening.

Above:
This computer-enhanced view of our globe without cloud cover shows the intensity of lights from the cities of Europe, the Middle East and Indian sub-continent compared with that of the sparsely developed continent of Africa.

Right:
In the middle of Siberian Russia lies Omsk, a city built astride the track of the Trans-Siberian Railway. Drifting snow and a low camera angle accentuate the grid-like pattern of the city in the "middle of nowhere."

NATURAL AND MAN-MADE BOUNDARIES

The boundaries between different nations often can be appreciated better from space than from the ground. Where there are political as well as natural boundaries it is even more evident. Often political boundaries lie along geographical features like rivers.

The Itaipu Dam Project is a joint Brazil-Argentine hydro-electric scheme that is the largest in the world. The dam at the bottom of the lakeshore is 6 miles long and 200ft high. Its output is about 12,600 megawatts.

River Parana

The boundary between Brazil (right) and Argentina is marked by farm fields on the Brazilian side and managed forest between the Argentinian border and the river.

THE BRAZIL-ARGENTINA BORDER

Iguassu Falls

The Igauanu river forms a natural boundary with the Parana river and they encompass two sides of a National park. Within its boundaries lie the spectacular *Carartas del Iguassu*, or Iguassu Falls which plunge down 270ft into a steep canyon.

Smoke from burning oil installations

WAR FROM THE AIR

Imaging from a remote sensor can track a tank in a desert or a platoon in a tundra. Similarly, the plume of oil smoke was tracked as soon as Saddam Hussein had lit the oil wells in his retreat from Kuwait in 1991 (opposite). Scientist could analyse the clouds, determine their chemical makeup, and warn of potential problems.

Kuwait City

Holes in the sky

See also:
- **The air around us** *p14*
- **El Niño** *p58*
- **Global weather** *p68*
- **Clouds and storms** *p70*

A THINNING SHIELD

There is a layer in the atmosphere, 12–13 miles above the Earth, that is rich in a kind of oxygen called ozone. This layer is important because it filters out much of the ultraviolet radiation from the sun.

Since the mid-1980s scientists have found that there is an annual thinning of this ozone layer, particularly over the Poles. The most obvious cause seems to be pollution by chemicals, particularly chlorofluocarbons (CFCs). Sunlight breaks down the CFCs in the atmosphere and the released chlorine reduces the filtering properties of the ozone. The increase in UV radiation that reaches us can lead to skin cancers.

THE EARTH'S climate is constantly changing. We need only look at the strata of ancient rocks, or the ice layers in Greenland, to tell that. Gases from volcanoes and hot springs continually change the composition of the atmosphere. But there is a mass of evidence to suggest that the climate is now changing much faster than normal. The agent of this change is ourselves. Industry and technology fill the atmosphere with pollutants, while chemical wastes are altering the physics and chemistry of the atmosphere itself. These changes are bound to affect our lives.

NO SMOKE WITHOUT FIRE

Erupting volcanoes, such as Mount Pinatubo and Mount St Helens, belch out immense quantities of gas, dust, and ash into the atmosphere. Vehicles, power stations, and factories further pollute the atmosphere by releasing sulfur dioxide and nitrogen oxide. These pollutants can be carried great distances by the winds, and are removed only by rain or snow.

Some of the chemicals released can dissolve in rainwater, forming a corrosive kind of rain known as "acid rain." This has had the effect of rotting crops, poisoning lakes, killing trees, and causing respiratory diseases.

THAT SINKING FEELING

Over the last 200 years or so, there has been a change in the atmosphere. Industry has generated carbon dioxide from the burning of fossil fuels, and other increased gases include methane and water vapor. All these together produce the "greenhouse effect."

These gases allow the sun's rays through to the Earth's surface, but the heat radiated from the surface is then trapped by the gases, so increasing the temperature on the Earth's

surface. On a worldwide scale this may produce global warming. One effect would be to melt the ice caps and raise the sea level. Low-lying areas such as Florida (*left*) would be very vulnerable to this.

AN EL NIÑO SIDESHOW

Early 1998 saw devastating fires in Borneo for the second year running, the result of "slash and burn" agriculture, in which areas of natural forest are burned to provide farming land. A simultaneous drought, as a result of the "El Niño effect," meant that the fires raged out of control. Satellite sensors showed the rise and fall of the atmospheric haze in South-east Asia over three months, causing severe health problems.

2 FEBRUARY 1998

21 MARCH 1998

22 APRIL 1998

Left:
The hole in the ozone layer was first detected by the British Antarctic Survey at Halley Bay in Antarctica in 1982. This first satellite image was taken in 1988 by NASA's satellite TOMS. Since then the hole has been enlarging.

Soiled waters

See also:
- **The air around us** *p14*
- **El Niño** *p58*
- **Global weather** *p68*
- **Clouds and storms** *p70*

Below:
Madagascar is running out of soil. It is being washed into the sea. The red stain in the water shows clearly in this shot from the space shuttle of the Betsiboka River outfall, with the Mozambique Channel at the top.

THE OCEAN has always been regarded as having an infinite capacity – a dustbin that could absorb anything, however too much rubbish was dumped in it.

Sadly, this has proved not to be true. The enormous volume of human garbage and industrial waste built up over the centuries is now altering the composition and quality of the sea.

The problem is most obvious in confined seas with poor circulation, such as the Mediterranean, and in areas bordering on busy ports and large cities. But recently, fears have also been expressed about the condition of even the deepest parts of the ocean floor.

A SPILL TOO MANY

Much of the world's economy is based on oil, which has to be transported by tanker from place to place. During the Arab-Israeli War in the 1960s a new generation of "supertankers" was built, to enable oil traffic to bypass the Suez Canal.

The first big accident involving an oil supertanker was the oil spill from the *Torrey Canyon* off Cornwall, England, in 1967.

Right:
On 24 March, 1989, the tanker Exxon Valdez *ran aground in Alaska, rupturing her tanks and spilling out crude oil. The oil slick that resulted polluted the shoreline, took years to clean up, and cost millions.*

Below:
The Straits of Hormuz, at the bottom of the Persian Gulf, sees 20 percent of the world's oil traffic pass through its waters. Oil slicks, debris, and waste discharges are all killing the marine environment.

Top:
Tanker spills are spectacular, but most pollution comes from discharge of machine waste. The wildlife suffers just the same.

BUSY CROSSROADS

The nature of sea traffic means that some areas are much busier than others. The English Channel, the Cape of Good Hope, the Malay Straits, and the Straits of Hormuz are some of the busier waterways in the world, and therefore the most vulnerable.

International agencies such as the Intergovernmental Maritime Consultative Organization have been set up to minimize human impact on such areas, by regulating sea traffic and advising on tanker design.

PART FOUR

Snapshots of our world

Fly by Earth –
Four global views show us how we
look from space

The Americas and the Eastern Pacific

THE TOPOGRAPHY of the Americas is one of the most varied to be found on this planet.

The northern parts of Canada lie in the Arctic, while the southern tip of South America was until recently (in geological time) joined to Antarctica.

North and Central America

North America occupies the northern part of the western hemisphere and has a core of ancient rock known as the Canadian Shield.

Huge mountain chains run down the eastern and western flanks of North America. The oldest are the Appalachian mountains in the east, formed some 400 million years ago. They have been worn away by

DEATH VALLEY in California USA is the lowest part of the American continent. In places the valley rises to over 10,000 ft but it is more famous for the fact that it is 230 ft below sea level.

The Amazon river stretches for 4,080 miles, is the world's second longest river and is surrounded by some of the most dense Equatorial rainforest in the world– it is also the most threatened.

wind and rain for so long that they are now much lower than the younger, sharp-crested Rocky Mountains to the west. Between lie the Great Plains – originally home to over 500 tribes of Native Americans, who were gradually ousted by immigrant white settlers. North America is rich in minerals and oil.

Central America, the thin ribbon of land that joins the continents, encompasses over 30 countries and many small islands with mountainous, volcanic landscapes.

South America

The world's fourth largest continent straddles the Equator and includes one of its richest resources – the Amazon rainforest. This mass of virgin forest is a major source of the world's oxygen and contains almost half of all the world's living

LAKE SUPERIOR is the second largest lake in the world and the biggest of the Great Lakes. These lakes were formed at the end of the Ice Age, when melting ice filled ground-out hollows.

species. The Amazon itself contains over one-fifth of the world's fresh water.

The Andes mountains run down the western seaboard of South America.

STAGGERING STATISTICS

1 **Highest point**
Aconcagua, Argentina 22,833ft

2 **Lowest point**
Death Valley, California, USA 282ft
below sea level

3 **Largest lake**
Lake Superior, Canada/USA
32,140 sq miles

4 **Longest river**
Amazon, Brazil 4,080 miles

CANADA

USA

HAWAII

GALAPAGOS
ISLANDS

BRAZIL

FRENCH
POLYNESIA

ARGENTINA

DEEP INSIDE the Andes stands the snow-shrouded peak of Aconcagua. This extinct volcano is South America's highest mountain.

Europe and Africa

Caspian Sea, and Aral Sea.

Europe
Europe is the second smallest continent in the world, but it has a complicated layout and an ancient geological history.

It stretches from the Ural mountains in the east, where it joined onto Asia some 300 million years ago, to the Atlantic shoreline. To the north are the mountains of Scotland and Norway, which are about 400 million years old. To the south are crumpled fold mountains that are still forming as Europe and Africa slowly slide past one another – the Atlas Mountains in the north of Africa, then Sicily, the Appenines, the Alps, and the Carpathians.

STAGGERING STATISTICS

① Highest point in Africa
Kilimanjaro, Kenya, 19,364ft

② Highest point in Europe
Mount Elbrus, Caucasus, 18,517ft

③ Lowest point
Lac Assal, Djibouti, 471ft below sea level

④ Longest river
Nile, longest in the world, 4,160 miles

THE NORTH and south continental landmasses were once separated by the mighty Tethys Ocean. That ocean has almost disappeared as Africa has slowly moved north-east toward Europe, squeezing and crumpling the mountains in between, and leaving only the "puddles" of the Mediterranean, Black Sea,

THE NORTH-ERNMOST part of Europe lies inside the Arctic Circle, where the conifer forests of Norway, Sweden, and Finland give way to icy plains. The whole of Scandinavia was covered with glaciers during the last Ice Age and the land is still rising, relieved of the great weight of ice.

The movement of Africa is slowly stretching Europe in an east-west direction, producing the rift valleys of the Rhône and the Rhine, and the North Sea oil fields. The complex arrangement of bays, lochs, peninsulas, fjords, and inlets gives Europe the longest coastline of any continent.

The climate is also complex, ranging from the balmy Mediterranean in the south, to the northern areas where the warm westerlies met the cold polar easterlies, creating unstable weather conditions. Eastern Europe, far from the sea, has a continental climate, with very hot summers and very cold winters.

Africa

Africa is about three times the size of Europe, built around chunks of ancient metamorphic rock. A system of rift valleys runs up the eastern side of the continent, marking a line where the continent will one day tear itself apart.

Madagascar has already gone, and one day East Africa may also become an island. The Great Rift Valley system continues up East Africa into Ethiopia and the Red Sea. This Rift Valley, formed over some five million years, is where mankind first evolved some two million years ago, spreading out to colonize the world.

Like two pieces of a jigsaw, the west coast of Africa reflects the eastern coast of South America, to which it was once joined.

Africa is crossed by the Equator, marked by tropical rainforest. On either side lies tropical grassland, and beyond that are belts of desert – the Sahara in the north and the Kalahari in the south. The extreme north and south have a Mediterranean-type climate.

THIS FALSE color Landsat image shows the Nile River with its delta, as well as Sinai and the Red Sea. The Red Sea is slowly widening as part of the Rift Valley system. In time it will link up with the Mediterranean, but not for many millions of years.

Asia, Australia, and the Western Pacific

THESE THREE vast areas, including two continents, cover half the globe.

Asia

Asia is the largest continent in the world, accounting for about one-third of the total land surface of the Earth. The islands of the East Indies stretch below the Equator, while the northern tip of Siberia lies within the Arctic Circle.

In the west, Asia has been joined to Europe along the Ural Mountains for some 300 million years. In the east it narrows to a point at the Bering Strait where it is only 53 miles from North America.

In the south it is almost joined to Africa, but the Red Sea is gradually widening, pushing the two continents apart.

The highest mountains in the world – the Himalayas – were formed a mere 50 million years ago, when the Indian plate moved north-ward and collided with the Asian plate, forcing the younger rocks upward. That movement is still taking place. The plate movement also crumpled up rocks to form the islands of the East Indies.

Along the eastern coast, the Pacific Ocean floor is slowly being drawn down under the continent, result-ing in the islands of Japan, the Philippines, the Kurile islands, and the Aleutians.

THE TIBETAN plateau behind the Himalayas is a windswept place. What agriculture is attempted there exists in river valleys such as the Yarlung Zang-bo Jiang, where winter wheat and barley are grown.

Australia

Australia is the largest island continent in the world. It was once joined to Antarctica, but broke off some 60 million years ago and drifted north-wards. It is still moving north, and eventually it will collide with Asia.

Australia lies across the Tropic of Capricorn, hence its interior desert and tropical grassland. The north has Equatorial rain-forest, while the south has a Mediterranean climate.

The east of Australia has a chain of mountains run-ning north to south, known as the Great Divid-ing Range. Most of the population lives in the coastal strip between these

STAGGERING STATISTICS

1. **Highest point**
   Everest 29,116ft

2. **Lowest point**
   Dead Sea
   1,293ft below sea level

3. **Largest lake, also the deepest in the world (5,710ft) and the oldest (50 million years)**
   Lake Baikal, Siberia 12,150 sq miles

4. **Longest river**
   Lena 2,730 miles. Empties into the Arctic in a 240-mile-wide delta

THE PACIFIC Ocean is littered with volcanic activity. This string of volcanic cones, outlined with cloud, is in Java, just north of Australia. Many of these volcanoes are still active.

THE KURILE Islands between Russia and Japan form part of the "Ring of Fire." Just west of these islands the sea floor plunges to its greatest depths on earth.

mountains and the sea. The only other notable range – the Olgas – lies in the center of Australia and includes the famous Ayers Rock.

Western Pacific

The volcanic islands of the Western Pacific form an arc from the Aleutian Islands and Japan to the Philippines and New Guinea, following the deep ocean trenches. Many of these volcanoes are still active, and form the famous "Ring of Fire."

A further series of volcanic island chains runs from New Guinea to Fiji. These are the remains of hotspot volcanoes.

This area is known as Melanesia. It was first colonized some 30,000 years ago by hunters from south-east Asia – the same aborigines who first colonized Australia.

The North and South Poles

THE POLAR REGIONS are the coldest places on Earth. Within the Arctic and Antarctic Circles are parts that sometimes get no sunlight at all and other places where in summer the sun never sets. At the Poles themselves there are six months of darkness followed by six months of daylight.

The North Pole
The North Pole lies in the Arctic Ocean. The ice cap floats in the ocean with pack ice and only a few scattered islands lying beneath it. The only landmass of any size is Greenland, which also has an ice cap. Glaciers along the coast produce thousands of icebergs every year. These icebergs travel south to Newfoundland in the Labrador Current, and are eventually melted by the Gulf Stream.

The North Pole, although so far from industrialized nations, suffers from pollution. DDT has been found in cod in the Barents Sea, and Caesium 137 from Chernobyl was found in northern Scandinavia.

The South Pole
At the South Pole lies the continent of Antarctica, twice the size of Australia. It is a typical continent with an old landmass at the center, and mountain ranges along the edges. Most of the landmass is covered in ice, and the

weight is so great that it presses down the interior below sea level. Only about one percent of the

Antarctic is free from ice, consisting mainly of mountains that protrude through the ice.

The few parts of the

Greenland is almost totally covered by an ice cap. If the ice melted then the land on which it rested would rise by about 3 ft.

coastal plain that are free from ice are cold and barren. However, the summer sunlight produces blooms of algae in the sea that attract vast shoals of fish. These fish in their turn are hunted by seals and flocks of penguins.

There are even active volcanoes in the Antarctic, including Mount Erebus, the most southerly active volcano in the world.

THE NORTH POLAR REGIONS

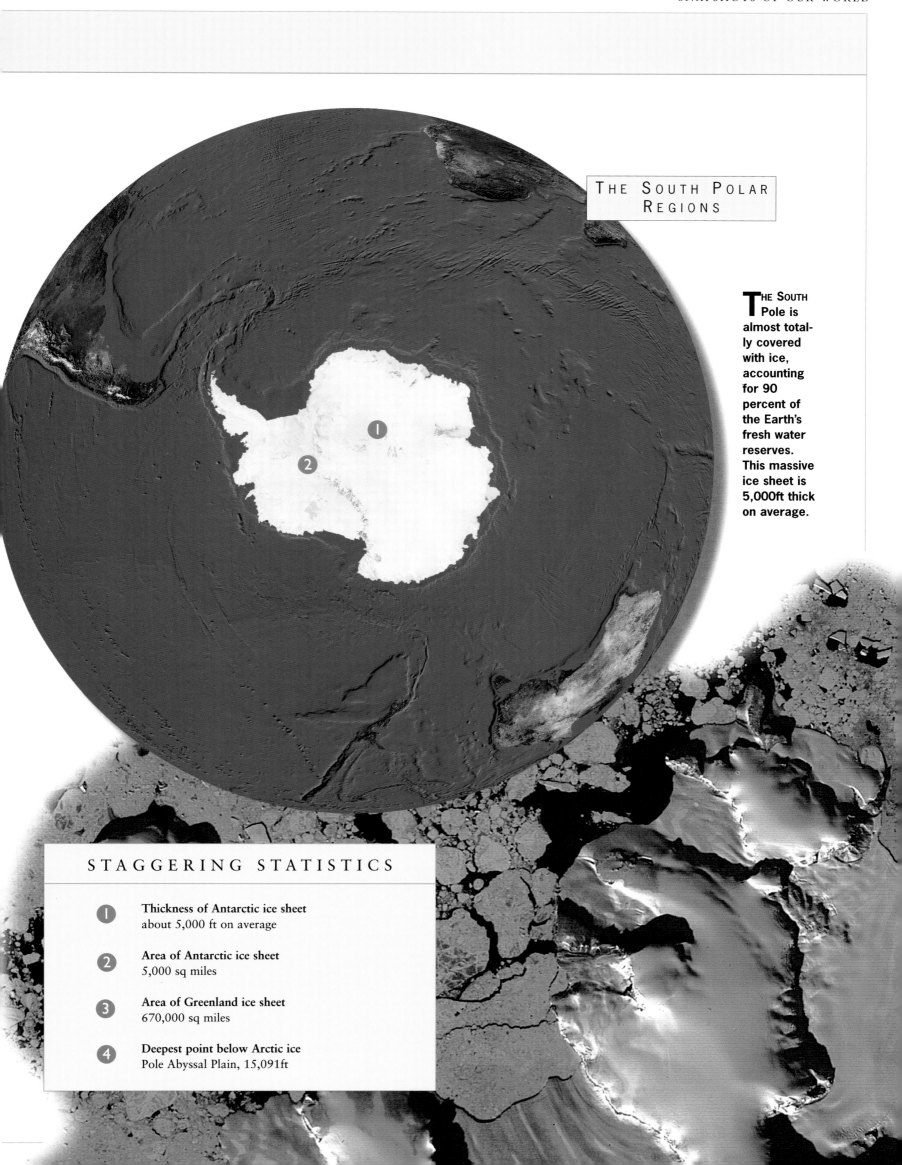

THE SOUTH
Pole is
almost total-
ly covered
with ice,
accounting
for 90
percent of
the Earth's
fresh water
reserves.
This massive
ice sheet is
5,000ft thick
on average.

STAGGERING STATISTICS

1 Thickness of Antarctic ice sheet
about 5,000 ft on average

2 Area of Antarctic ice sheet
5,000 sq miles

3 Area of Greenland ice sheet
670,000 sq miles

4 Deepest point below Arctic ice
Pole Abyssal Plain, 15,091ft

Glossary

A

Abyssal plain
The flat bed of the ocean between the continents, from which the *ocean ridges* rise, and which dips into the *continental trenches*. The abyssal plain is between 11,500 and 18,200 ft deep and lies in permanent darkness.

Acid rain
Rain that has become acidic because of chemicals dissolved from the atmosphere. A common cause of acid rain is waste gases given off by factories which can damage crops and poison groundwater downwind from the source of pollution. Acid rain is also caused naturally by the gases erupted from *volcanoes*.

Alluvium
Loose material, such as sand, mud, or silt, that is deposited by rivers and streams. Some of the most fertile farmland is formed on alluvium deposited by rivers in flood.

Andesitic volcano
A *volcano* that erupts andesitic *lava*, which is relatively rich in the mineral silica. This makes the lava thick and easily solidified. Such volcanoes are formed through the action of *plate tectonics*, where one plate is overriding another. The *magma* is derived from molten plate material and the eruptions tend to be very violent and explosive, in contrast to *basaltic volcanoes*.

Arctic Circle
The theoretical line, at a latitude of 66°30 North, within which the sun does not rise during at least one day of the year, and does set during at least one day. Its equivalent in the southern hemisphere is the Antarctic Circle.

Asteroid
A body of rock, smaller than a planet or a moon, that orbits the sun in the Solar System. Asteroids are sometimes called "planetoids."

Asthenosphere
A layer within the Earth's *mantle* that is fairly soft. It is the lubricating layer on which the Earth's plates move during the process of *plate tectonics*. The layer that comprises the plates is called the *lithosphere*.

Atoll
A ring-shaped coral reef. Atolls form when islands gradually subside, allowing any coral reef around the edge to grow, keeping pace with the rate of subsidence. The lagoon in the middle represents the original area of the island.

B

Basalt
A dark, fine-grained, *igneous rock*. It erupts from fissures in volcanoes that do not erupt explosively, and then cools and hardens. Basaltic *lava* is usually erupted at the bottom of the ocean. It can form lava fields thousands of feet thick.

Basaltic volcano
A *volcano* that erupts basaltic *lava*. Basaltic volcanoes are broad and flat as the lava tends to flow some distance and spread out before solidifying into *basalt* rock. These volcanoes are found where new plates are being generated. The *magma* is low in silica, derived from the *mantle*, and produces gentle eruptions.

Breaker
An ocean wave that curls over when it reaches shallow water and breaks into surf on the shore.

British Antarctic Survey
An institute of Britain's Natural Environment Research Council, specializing in the study of Antarctica.

C

Calcite
The mineral calcium carbonate – $CaCO_3$. It is easily broken down by the action of acid in rainwater. It is the principal ingredient of limestone and its instability accounts for the characteristic erosion patterns of limestone landscapes.

Caldera
A very large *crater* caused by the inward collapse of a *volcano* into its *magma* chamber. If the volcano is extinct the crater will be filled with water,

Canyon
A deep gorge cut in the rock by a stream. Canyons are often found in arid areas subjected to heavy flash floods at certain times of the year, such as the south-west of the United States.

Cavern
A cave, particularly one formed by solution in a *limestone* terrain.

Chlorofluocarbon (CFC)
A gaseous substance, a compound of chlorine, fluorine, and carbon, used in many industrial processes. It is not easily broken down, and its buildup in the atmosphere can lead to pollution problems as it damages the *ozone layer*.

Cirque
An armchair-shaped hollow in the side of a mountain with a glacier. The cirque is the place where the glacier originated, the great weight of the accumulation of snow and ice grinding out the hollow. Cirque is a French term,

originally applying to the Alps. In the Scottish Highlands the feature is called a corrie, and in the Welsh mountains a cwm.

Climate
The metereological conditions of an area, averaged out over a long period of time. This differs from weather, in that weather is the day to day variation in the climate of an area.

Conglomerate
A *sedimentary rock* consisting of large rounded fragments, like a fossilized shingle beach.

Coniferous
Description of a tree that bears its seeds in cones. Coniferous trees usually have leaves in the form of needles. Pine, fir and spruce are typical coniferous trees.

Continent
A very large landmass.

Continental shelf
The submerged edge of a continent, covered by seawater to a depth of about 400 ft. Beyond this is the continental slope, where the sea becomes deeper very rapidly.

Convection
The process whereby a gas or liquid moves upward when it becomes warm and less dense, and the cooler, denser portion flows in to take its place.

Coral
A kind of tiny marine animal without a backbone. Corals are sedentary, extracting calcium carbonate from sea water to make limy shells. Hundreds of thousands of coral shells built up on one another form a reef.

Core
The innermost part of the Earth's structure. It is mostly

made of iron and consists of two parts – an inner core that is solid, and an outer core that is liquid.

Coriolis effect
The process by which anything moving towards the Equator, such as the wind, is deflected to the west, and anything moving away from the Equator is deflected to the east. The effect is caused by the rotation of the Earth.

Crater
A circular depression formed at the top of an erupting volcano. It can also be caused by the impact of a *meteorite*.

Crevasse
A deep crack, especially in the surface of a glacier. The rigid surface of a glacier cracks and splits as the glacier flows round a sharp corner of its valley, or over a hump on the valley floor.

Crust
The topmost layer of the Earth's structure. It is made of the lightest rocky material and surrounds the *mantle*. Two types of crust are recognized – oceanic crust and continental crust. Oceanic crust is denser and forms the floors of the oceans. The continental crust is the only part of the Earth's structure we normally see, and is lighter than the oceanic crust. Individual masses of the continental crust form the continents and are embedded in the oceanic crust. The plates that take part in *plate tectonics* consist of the crust and the topmost layer of the *mantle*.

Crystal
A naturally formed piece of a mineral that has a specific shape. This shape reflects the arrangement of atoms in the mineral, just as the rectangular shape of a house reflects the shape of the bricks.

D

Deciduous
Describes a tree that loses its leaves in the fall and grows new ones in spring, such as oak and ash.

Delta
An area of *deposition* at the mouth of a river, where sandy material washed down by the river piles up as sandbanks, and the river has to cut its own channels through. A delta forms where there are no sea currents to wash the deposited material away.

Deposition
The process by which material washed along by a river or a stream settles on the bottom when the current slackens, to build up beds of *sediment*.

E

Ecosphere
In an astronomical sense, the theoretical region around the Sun in which it is possible for life as we know it to exist. Often used in the biological sense as meaning the Earth and the region within the atmosphere.

Ejecta
The broken material thrown out by a *volcano* or blasted out by the impact of a *meteorite*.

El Niño
A pattern of weather caused by the disruption of the normal flow of the prevailing winds and ocean currents in the Pacific Ocean. It happens every few years, with disastrous effects.

Epicentre
The point on the Earth's surface directly above the focus of an earthquake. Normally the greatest damage is done there.

Equator
The theoretical line drawn around the Earth at latitude 0°.

Erosion
The breaking down of rocks and landforms by the natural processes of weather, or by river currents or the pounding of waves.

F

Fjord
A long, deep, narrow inlet from the ocean, bounded by steep cliffs. Fjords are carved by the action of glaciers and are common on the west coast of Norway.

Fossil
The remains of a plant or animal found preserved in rocks. Most fossils are found in *sedimentary rock*.

G

Glacier
A mass of ice that builds up on land by repeated snowfalls and then moves slowly downhill with the effect of gravity.

Gondwana
The supercontinent that existed in the southern hemisphere up to about 50 million years ago. It comprised South America, Africa, India, Australia and Antarctica. It gradually split up and the continents slowly moved to their present positions.

Granite
An *igneous rock* consisting of large *crystals*, and containing a high proportion of silica, in the form of the *mineral* quartz.

Greenhouse effect
The warming of the Earth's surface due to the changing composition of the atmosphere, allowing the sun's rays in, but preventing excess heat from being radiated out.

Grike
A joint in a slab of *limestone* widened by the effect of *erosion* and weathering.

Groundwater
Water found under the surface of the Earth. Much of the rainwater that falls sinks into the ground, soaking the soil and accumulating at depth. At a certain depth the soil and rocks become saturated with water and can hold no more. This is known as the zone of saturation, and the top level of this is known as the water table.

Gyre
A vast circular movement of ocean currents.

I

Ice age
A time when the Earth's climate was cooler and the *ice sheets* and *glaciers* were more extensive than they are at present. The end of the last Ice Age was about 20,000 years ago.

Ice cap
A glacier that is not confined to a valley, but covers a large continental area. Such caps are found in Antarctica and Greenland, and also on the Arctic ocean. Unlike valley glaciers where the movement is downhill, the movement of an ice cap is outwards as new ice accumulates from snowfalls in the center. The terms ice cap and ice sheet are often used interchangeably.

Ice sheet
A glacier that covers a wide area of land, rather than being confined in a valley.

Igneous rock
One of the three main kinds of rock that make up the Earth's crust. It is formed when hot molten material such as *magma* cools and solidifies.

Glossary/2

Island arc
A string of volcanic islands in the shape of an arc, formed on the inside curve of an *ocean trench* through the action of *plate tectonics*.

J

Jet stream
A particularly strong wind found in the stratosphere in mid-latitudes, blowing eastward. It can reach speeds of 300 mph. It is a result of the circulation pattern of the atmosphere around the globe, and is often sought out by long-distance airline pilots to assist their eastward passage.

K

Karst
A very dry landscape form found in a region of *limestone*. This rock dissolves easily on exposure, particularly through the effects of *acid rain*. Joints or cracks in the the rock are dissolved into wide openings – *grikes* – leaving the intervening areas of rock as upstanding blocks called "clints." Karst is named for the area in the former Yugoslavia where the landform is common.

L

Lagoon
A shallow area of seawater partly or totally cut off from the sea by a barrier, such as a coral reef.

Lava
Molten rocky material, also known as *magma*, erupted from a *volcano*. It then cools and hardens on the Earth's surface. Basaltic lava is quite runny ands flows for long distances before solidifying. Andesitic lava is stiff and easily solidified, and so does not flow very far.

Levee
A raised bank along the sides of a river, built up from sediment deposited during successive floods.

Limestone
A *sedimentary rock* consisting mostly of the *mineral calcite*.

Lithosphere
The outer shell of the Earth that forms the tectonic plates. It is comprised of the *crust* and the topmost section of the *mantle*. It is solid and moves about on the softer *asthenosphere* below.

Longshore drift
An effect of a sea current in which sand and pebbles are transported in one direction along a beach. The effect results in *sand bars*, sand spits, and *tombolos*.

M

Magma
Molten rock that exists below the surface of the Earth. It is composed largely of silicate, with dissolved gases. When it erupts at the surface through volcanic action it becomes known as *lava*.

Mantle
The part of the Earth's structure that lies between the *core* and the *crust*. The mantle comprises the greatest proportion of the Earth's volume. It is made of a stony material and is solid, except for a soft layer close to the outside. This soft layer provides the lubrication that allows the outermost part of the Earth to move about in the process of *plate tectonics*.

Marble
A *metamorphic rock* formed when *limestone* is subjected to heat.

Meander
A loop formed in a slow-moving river as it crosses a flood plain. As the river winds through sediments deposited on the valley floor the current is always faster on the outside of the curves eroding the bank away. On the inside of the curve, eroded material being carried along is deposited as a beach. In this way the curve of the river extends itself, known as meandering.

Mediterranean-type climate
A climate characterized by warm wet westerly winds in winter and hot dry summers. South Africa, Southern Australia, parts of Chile and California experience a Mediterranean climate as well as the Mediterranean countries.

Metamorphic rock
A *rock* that forms when a pre-existing rock is heated or crushed so much that its *mineral* content changes. In this process it is important that the rock does not melt, otherwise the result would be an *igneous rock*.

Meteorite
A lump of rocky or metallic matter in space. Sometimes a meteorite will fall through the atmosphere and strike the Earth. The glowing trail produced by this fall is called a meteor.

Mineral
One of the constituents of a rock. A naturally formed substance that has a particular chemical composition. In their purest forms minerals form crystals. A rock may be made up of a number of different crystals.

N

NASA
National Aeronautics and Space Administration, established by the United States in 1958 to administer space exploration.

Neap tide
The tidal condition that occurs twice a month when the gravitational influence of the sun and the moon are pulling at right angles to one another. During neap tides there is only a small tidal range, with the high tides being relatively low, and the low tides relatively high. The opposite condition is the *spring tide*.

O

Ocean ridge
A ridge formed along the ocean floor by the upwelling of molten material from below the crust. This is where new plates are formed in the process of *plate tectonics*.

Ocean trench
Elongated depression in the ocean floor. It is formed by the process of *plate tectonics*, at the site where an old plate is destroyed as it slips down below the one next to it.

Oil trap
A rock structure underground that gathers and concentrates petroleum. Oil geologists spend much of their time looking for oil traps.

Ozone layer
A layer in theEarth's atmosphere that is particularly rich in a type of oxygen called ozone. It is important to life on Earth as it helps to filter out harmful rays from the Sun. Pollution by industrial gases tends to break down the ozone layer.

Ox-bow lake
A curved lake formed from a *meander* in a river that has gradually been cut off by deposits of sediment.

P

Peninsula
A narrow piece of land that stretches into the sea or a large lake: an "almost island."

Permafrost
The phenomenon whereby a layer of frozen soil underground does not thaw even during the summer. At high latitudes this results in waterlogged landscapes, called tundra, where the meltwater from the surface cannot drain away.

Pingo
A landscape feature associated with *permafrost*, consisting of an underground "blister" of ice that expands and pushes up into a soil-covered mound. Pingoes can be up to 200 ft high.

Plate tectonics
The movement of the Earth's surface as a series of plates, constantly being created at one side (in *ocean ridges*) and destroyed at the other (in *ocean trenches)*. These plates are constantly moving, and cause earthquakes and mountain ranges where they collide.

R

Reef
A body of rock that lies just below the surface of the water. *Corals* can form reefs.

Rift valley
A valley formed as the Earth's crust stretches, and an area of land subsides between cracks or faults.

Rock cycle
The process whereby rocks are broken down by the force of *erosion*, the debris transported by rivers, glaciers, wind, sea currents, and so on. This debris is eventually deposited, buried and turned into other rocks. In other parts of the process rocks are heated and compressed in the depths of the Earth to become new rocks, or rocks are melted and resolidified into new rocks.

S

Sand bar
A deposit of sand, either underwater or just breaking the surface as a sandy island, formed by the movement of waves and sea currents.

Savanna
Dry tropical grassland with few trees. It borders the Equatorial forests.

Schist
A *metamorphic rock* whose twisted shape and flattened crystals show the pressure under which it was formed.

Sediment
Loose rocky material eroded from the land and deposited on a sea floor, river bed or desert basin.

Sedimentary rock
A rock formed when sediment is laid down by the process of erosion, and then compressed, and the particles cemented together.

Shield area
A region of ancient *metamorphic rocks* found in the heart of a continent. They are given individual names, such as the Canadian Shield and the Baltic Shield.

Shale
A fine-grained *sedimentary rock* formed by the solidification of mud.

Soil
The mixture of broken rocky material and plant debris that forms the surface layer of the Earth.

Solstice
The time of the year when the sun is at its highest point or its lowest point in the sky.

Spring tide
The tidal condition that occurs twice a month when the gravitational influence of the sun and the moon are pulling in the same direction. During spring tides there is a large tidal range, with the high tides being particularly high and the low tides particularly low. The opposite condition is the neap tide. The name is misleading, as the spring tide has nothing to do with the season of spring.

Strata
The layers in which sedimentary rocks form.

Sub-continent
An area of land that has the characteristics of a continent but is still attached to a larger landmass. India is an example.

Supercontinent
A very large continent, usually formed by the coming together of individual continents during the process of *plate tectonics*. A supercontinent may eventually break up into smaller ones, again by means of *plate tectonics*.

T

Tectonic
To do with the movement of the Earth's surface and the building of mountains.

Tombolo
An island that is attached to the land by a *sand bar*.

Trade winds
The prevailing winds that blow towards the Equator. They are generated by the warm air rising over the hottest area of the Earth, and cooler air to the north and south sweeping in to take its place. They do not blow due north and south but are deflected to the west because of the *Coriolis effect*.

Tundra
In the northern hemisphere the northernmost icy plains covered with snow and ice thaw out during the brief summer. The soil at depth remains frozen, known as *permafrost*, so the meltwater on the surface cannot drain away. The result is a treeless landscape of lakes and marshes, known as tundra.

Typhoon
The local name for a hurricane in the Indian Ocean or China Sea.

U

UTC
Universal Time Coordinated. An internationally agreed basis for timekeeping, introduced in 1972 and based on International Atomic Time, by means of atomic clocks and satellites.

V

Volcano
The vent through which *lava* and *ejecta* are erupted during a *tectonic* upheaval. The material builds up around the vent to form a mountain, usually with a *crater* in the top. There are two kinds of volcano, broad, flat *basaltic volcanoes* , and steep-sided conical *andesitic volcanoes*.

W

Water cycle
The constant movement of water from the oceans through evaporation, into the atmosphere as vapor, onto the land as rain, and back to the oceans through the movement of rivers.

Index

Acknowledgments

Picture credits

l=left, *r*=right, *t*=top, *c*=center, *b*=bottom

Front cover lt Jim Robins, *inset* Spot Image, *b* Science Photo Library; *back cover t* GSFC/NASA, *b* NASA ; *front endpaper* NASA; 1 NASA/Science Photo Library; 2-3 NASA/Science Photo Library; 4-5 WorldSat; 6 NASA/Science Photo Library; 7 NASA; 8 *l* AND, *r* Science Photo Library, *b* NASA; 9 Planet Earth Pictures; 10 *lc* NASA, *lb* NASA/Science Photo Library, 11 *rl* NASA, *rb* GSFC/NASA; 12 *tl* AND, *bl* NASA/Science Photo Library, *c* AND, 13 *t* AND, *b* AND; 14 *l* NASA/Science Photo Library, *bl* AND, *bc* NASA , 15 *t* F Zullo/Science Photo Library, *r* Julian Baker; 16 *t* Julian Baker, *b* BP/NRSC/Science Photo Library; 17 *t* Julian Baker, WorldSat, *c* Planet Earth Pictures, *b* Julian Baker; 17 WorldSat; 18 *r* AND; 19 *bl* AND, *br* ZEFA; 20 *l* NASA, *ct* NASA, *cb* NASA, *r* WorldSat; 21 *tc* WorldSat, *tr* Planet Earth Pictures, *c* WorldSat, *b* Mark Lawson; 22 WorldSat; 23 *c* NASA, *t* Julian Baker, *cb* Southampton Oceanography Centre, *r* NASA; 24 *lc* Planet Earth Pictures/Pascal Tournaire, *lb* WorldSat, *ct* NASA, *ctr* Landsat, *cl* NASA, *cr* NASA ; 25 *t* Julian Baker, *cb* WorldSat, *rt* NASA, *rc* NASA; 26 *tl* David Parker/Science Photo Library, *tr* Martin Bond/Science Photo Library, *lc* Massonet *et al*/CNES/Science Photo Library; 27 *t* Julian Baker, *c* NASA, *bl* Popperphoto, *br* Peter Menzel/Science Photo Library; 28 *t* NASA, *b* Planet Earth Pictures/John Lythgoe; 29 *l* Adam Hart-Davis/Science Photo Library, *rt* Planet Earth Pictures, *rc* Planet Earth Pictures, *r* Natural History Museum, *rb* NASA; 30 *t* GSFC/NOAA, *b* AND; 31 *t* Julian Baker, *c* NASA, *rb* François Gohier/Science Photo Library; 32 *l* NASA, *b* Julian Baker *c* Natural History Museum; 33 *r* NASA, *c* AND; 34 *t* NASA, *b* Landsat; 35 *l* Julian Baker, *r* AND, *cr* AND, *bl* Planet Earth Pictures/Ken Vaughan; 36 Landsat/Science Picture Library; 37 NASA; 38 NASA, 39 *c* NASA, *l* NASA, *tr* Julian Baker; 40 *l* WorldSat, *b* Science Picture Library, *r* AND; 41 *l* NASA, *b* AND, *r* NASA; 42 *l* NASA, *br* Julian Baker; 43 *t* NASA, *b* NASA; 44 *l* NASA; 45 *t* Julian Baker, *r* Science Photo Library, *b* Julian Baker; 46 *t* NASA, *b* Planet Earth Pictures/Jean Paul Navicet; 47 *r* Landsat, *b* AND; 48 *l* WorldSat, *t* NRSC/Science Picture Library, *b* Planet Earth Pictures/Jonathon Scott , 49 *l* NASA, *lc* Landsat, *c* Landsat, *cr* NASA, *bc* Julian Baker, *b* NASA, *r* Snow and Ice Center/University of Colorado at Boulder; 50 *l* Spot Image, *b* AND, *c* NASA; 51 *l* Julian Baker, *rt* A. C. Twomey/Science Photo Library; 52 *l* WorldSat, *b* AND; 53 *t* AND, *b* Julian Baker; 54 *t* Landsat, *r* Landsat, *b* WorldSat; 55 *l* Planet Earth Pictures, *c* AND, *r* Julian Baker, *b* Planet Earth Pictures; 56 *l* NASA, *c* NASA, *r* NASA; 57 *l* AND, *r* NASA; 58 *l* GSFC/NASA, *l* Planet Earth Pictures, *c* NASA; 59 *t* AND, *b* GSFC/NASA; 60 NASA; 61 *t* Julian Baker, *r* AND, *bl* Planet Earth Pictures, *r* Planet Earth Pictures/ Alex Williams; 62 WorldSat; 63 *l* Julian Baker, *r* NASA, *b* Landsat; 64 NASA; 65 *t* Julian Baker, *c* NASA, *b* Planet Earth Pictures/Gary Bell; 66 NASA; 67 NASA; 68 *l* AND, *b* NASA; 69 *c* NOAA/NASA, *r* Julian Baker, *b* NASA; 70 *t* NASA, *c* NASA, *b* NASA, *r* NASA; 71 *t* Julian Baker, *b* Planet Earth Pictures/ David Ponton; 72 *t* GSFC/Science Photo Library, *b* NOAA/NASA; 73 Julian Baker, *r* GSFC/NASA, *cb* Science Photo Library *b* AND; 74 *l* NASA/Science Photo Library, *b* NASA; 75 *c* Landsat, *b* NASA; 76 *l* NOAA/Science Photo Library; 77 *l* NOAA/NASA, *c* NASA/Science Photo Library, *b* NOAA/NASA; 79 *l* NASA, *r* S Fraser/Science Photo Library, *b* V Vick/Science Photo Library; 80 NASA/Science Photo Library; 82 *t* NASA, *c* NASA, *b* Science Photo Library; 83 *c* WorldSat, *r* AND, *b* NASA; 84 *l* WorldSat, *c* WorldSat; 85 *t* AND, *b* ESI/Science Photo Library; 86 *t* AND, *c* NASA; 87 *c* WorldSat, *r* NASA, *b* NASA; 88 *t* NASA, *c* WorldSat; 89 *c* WorldSat, *b* Spot Image; 96 WorldSat; *back endpaper* NASA.